Bad Blood

COLM TÓIBÍN was born in Ireland in 1955. He is the author of seven novels, most recently *Brooklyn*, the 2009 Costa Novel of the Year, *The Master*, which was shortlisted for the 2004 Man Booker Prize and winner of the *LA Times* Book Prize and the IMPAC Book Award, and *The Blackwater Lightship*, which was shortlisted for the 1999 Booker Prize and the 2001 IMPAC Award. His non-fiction includes *Bad Blood*, *Homage to Barcelona*, *The Sign of the Cross* and *Love in a Dark Time*. He is also the author of two short-story collections, *Mothers and Sons*, which was awarded the inaugural Edge Hill Prize, and *The Empty Family*, which was shortlisted for the 2011 Frank O'Connor International Short Story Award. His work has been translated into seventeen languages. He lives in Dublin.

Also by Colm Tóibín

COLM TÓIBÍN

Bad Blood

A WALK ALONG THE
IRISH BORDER

PICADOR

Originally published 1987 as *Walking Along The Border* with photographs by Tony O'Shea
by Queen Anne Press, a division of Macdonald & Co (Publishers) Ltd

First published 1994 by Vintage, a division of the Random House Group

First published by Picador 2001
an imprint of Pan Macmillan
20 New Wharf Road, London N1 9RR
Associated companies throughout the world
www.panmacmillan.com

ISBN 978-0-330-37358-6

A CIP catalogue record for this book is available from
the British Library.

Typeset by Intype London Ltd
Printed in the UK by CPI Group (UK) Ltd, Croydon CR0 4YY

Visit **www.picador.com** to read more about all our books
and to buy them. You will also find features, author interviews and
news of any author events, and you can sign up for e-newsletters
so that you're always first to hear about our new releases.

TO MY MOTHER

Contents

Contents

Acknowledgements

Acknowledgement is made to Faber & Faber and Seamus Heaney for permission to quote from 'Hercules and Antaeus' and from 'North'; to Victor Gollancz for permission to quote from Eugene McCabe's *Heritage*; to Methuen for permission to quote from *Pig In The Middle: The Army in Northern Ireland* by Desmond Hammill.

There are many people to thank; most of them are mentioned in the book, but there are others and they include: Aidan Dunne, who drew the map; David McKenna and Fintan O'Toole who read the manuscript; Ian Hill of the Northern Ireland Tourist Board; Edward Mulhall, Cathal Goan and Pat Kenny of RTE; Jim Cusack and Helen Shaw of *The Irish Times*; Obbie McCormack; Finnian Ferris; Des Smith who provided shelter; and David Neligan for his dentistry. Special thanks are due to Bernard and Mary Loughlin of the Tyrone Guthrie Centre at Annaghmakerrig.

1

A Bed for the Night

I walked out of Derry towards the border on a beautiful, cloudless afternoon, past the broken-down public houses, past the abandoned shirt factory and the new housing estates and the sailing boats on the Foyle. It was Saturday. I was wearing a rucksack. When I crossed the border I would turn right and take the road to Lifford.

In half an hour I would be in the Republic of Ireland where the price of petrol would be much higher, where the price of drink would be a constant source of discussion and where just about everything else – new cars, hi-fi, televisions, videos – cost more than in the North.

The river widened. There was a smell of cut grass. Men were playing golf on the other side of the river; down below the road there were boys fishing.

The soldier at the border stepped out from his hut as I came towards him.

'Walking, sir,' he said to me.

'I am,' I said.

'Where are you going, sir?' he asked me.

'To Lifford,' I said.

'You turn there, sir,' he said, pointing to the road.

'How far is it?' I asked.

'I don't know sir, ten miles, twenty miles.'

I walked on towards the customs posts. The first one, which belonged to Her Majesty, was closed up. No one would dream of smuggling from the South into the North. The Irish customs official sat in the second hut, waving each car by. They were all locals, he said, he knew them; there was no point in stopping them, it only annoyed them. They were probably just driving over to get cheap petrol.

Failte go Dun na nGall the sign said, 'Welcome to Donegal'. It was getting warmer, I could see the Foyle again in the distance. What I found odd was the opulence of the houses, the size of the fields, the sense of good, rich land. I had taken this road on the Republic's side of the Foyle because I thought it would be quieter. I also thought the land would be poor. I was expecting dry stone walls and wet pasture land with small cottages.

As I moved beyond the village of Carrigans, where three men talked in a pub about the price of drink (one having gone through £32 on New Year's Day), down to St Johnston, I began to notice the outhouses behind the farmhouses, how beautiful the stonework was, how well painted the woodwork was. I passed by farm after farm, noticing the well-trimmed hedges, the big houses, the huge fields used for silage or tillage, the large herds of cows in other fields; above all the outhouses.

I had a drink in the next village, St Johnston, and, since every small group in the pub made sure that no one else could hear what they were talking about, I finished up quickly and took a walk around the town. On the right-hand side stood the Orange Hall, painted in bright colours. The Orange Hall explained the well-kept farmhouses and big farms. This, though in the South, was Protestant territory.

'Is the hall used much?' I asked a passer-by.

'It's used a bit for bowling,' he said.

The sound of a band could be heard in the distance and as I moved down the street I caught sight of an accordion and pipe band, with several cars in front, and I could hear a version of *When the Saints Go Marching In* being played. The band was led by a boy carrying the Irish flag; people had come out from the pubs and the houses and stood watching as the parade passed by. It was a school band and mixed tunes such as *Amazing Grace* with well-known Republican anthems like *Roddy McCorley*:

O Ireland, Mother Ireland, you love them still the best
The fearless brave who fighting fell upon your hapless breast.

I decided to visit Toland's pub and have a pint, it was getting near six o'clock and I was tired of walking. If Lifford was ten miles away, then I could be there by ten o'clock. I would be tired, dog tired, but I could rest a few days, and if there was a festival on, as the women behind the bar in Toland's confirmed that there was, I could join in the festivities.

The women behind the bar began to interrogate me: Where was I from? Where did I live? How had I made my way to St Johnston? The clientele ranged around the horseshoe-shaped bar listened carefully and when I said I had walked they drew in their breath. From Derry? Walked? And was I not tired? I was, I said.

The two young men on my right at the bar disappeared to get a guitar and were away for some time. In their absence a smallish man with red hair in the corner, who had been watching me very attentively, was prevailed upon to sing. He took a huge gulp of his drink, cleared his throat and began an extremely heartfelt and high-pitched version of *Nobody's Child* with his eyes closed.

There was a thorn in his side, however, in the guise of an old man, who was drunk, and couldn't stop himself interrupting with comments which I was not able to make out. The woman behind the bar told him to stop and we listened as best we could to the song. As soon as the red-headed man had finished the old man started up. This time I had no difficulty understanding him. His song was about an Orangeman who went to Cavan where he met the devil. It was directed at the previous singer, who, from his protest at the song, I took to be an Orangeman, or at least a Protestant. The women behind the bar tried to stop the old man, but he had to finish the song, in which the Orangeman ended up in a black hole.

Outside, the summer afternoon was fading fast over the Foyle. It was time to go. There would be plenty of traffic, they said, I'd have no trouble getting a lift.

I went out and stood on the road. I had made certain arrangements with myself about walking. I had made rules. All progress along the border must be on foot, I had agreed. If I wanted to go and see something that was off my route I could do so by taxi or I could hitch a lift, but every move towards my ultimate destination, Newry, must be on foot, except if there was danger, and then I would do anything – hire a helicopter if necessary – to get out fast.

This meant that I could march into Lifford tonight, or I could stay somewhere along the way. The woman behind the bar, however, didn't believe that there was a boarding house between St Johnston and Lifford. I passed a church and graveyard facing the Foyle and went to look at the gravestones and the Protestant names: Roulston, McCracken, Barr, Moody, Hanna, Buchanan. 'This congregation founded in 1726', a notice said. The church was like a New England church. It had been built in 1849 and re-built in 1984, having been struck by lightning.

The road began to deteriorate. Twilight. The pink sun was going down against the hills. Dotted along the road were new bungalows with Spanish arches and multi-coloured brickwork as well as picture windows and tiled roofs. But the area, despite the odd patch of bogland, was still full of huge old houses, flat, fertile fields, large holdings. On gate after gate the signs read: 'Beware of Alsatian Dog'. Even some of the smaller cottages had the sign up.

Cars began to speed along the road towards Lifford, and for half an hour cars came from the opposite direction as well; they had been at the dog racing in Lifford. I had to be careful walking on the narrow road. The evening was settling in, and there was a white mist on the hills above the Foyle. Black beetles were crawling out from low ditches. I tried not to walk on them. Coloured lights flickered from the mast on the opposite hill.

It was half past twelve when I arrived in Lifford and the pubs were still open, opening hours had been extended due to the festival. The hotel, however, was closed up. It had closed a few months previously and there was talk that it would never open again: business was bad. There were a few bed and breakfast houses in the town and I was directed to these but they were all full. There was only one other place, someone said, but they thought it was full too. But I should go and try, they said.

I went and tried. I was tired and I would have slept in a hole in the wall. My feet were like two concrete blocks full of frayed muscles. I rang the bell of the house but there was no reply. I stood there for a while until a Garda car with several women in the back arrived and stopped outside the house; one of the women got out and said she was the proprietor. I explained my plight to her and she explained to me that the Gardaí, the police of the Republic, were giving herself and her friends a lift to a dance a few miles away. The Gardaí were looking out at me. I could stay the night, if I wanted, she wouldn't see me stuck, but I would have to sleep on a sofa. I said that was fine. She was in her late thirties, and seemed very friendly and genuinely concerned that I should have somewhere to stay.

Why didn't I come to the dance with herself and her friend? I told her about my feet. She said I should drop my bag and come to the dance as her child was asleep in the house and her aunt and her aunt's son were coming to babysit until she came back from the dance. I said that was all right with me, I would just go to bed. But that was the problem, she then told me, there was only one room where they could sit and that was where the sofa was.

The Gardaí had become impatient, and began to blow the horn of the car. I told her I would be happy if I had somewhere to sit down and at that very moment the aunt and the aunt's son arrived. The woman said she'd see me later and went to rejoin her friends in the Garda car. I was now at the mercy of her aunt and her aunt's son. I looked at them. I wanted to sleep in the room they wanted to sit in. The son turned on the television, the aunt went to make tea. When she came back I suggested to her as politely as I could that she and her son could go home and I would babysit.

'And have the child wake up and see you?' she peered at me.

'Well, if you told me what to do,' I said feebly.

'You'll just have to wait now until the dance is over,' she said firmly. 'The child would get an awful fright,' she said, looking over at me again. She poured the tea and her son switched the television from channel to channel. It was past one in the morning and there was only tennis on the box. 'We'll not bother with that,' he said and turned it off. We were now left to our own devices. We discussed the festival, the closing of the hotel, my birthplace, my business, until the aunt asked: 'Do you do the amusements?' I didn't know what she meant. 'The amusements,' she repeated, and her son examined me carefully to see what I would say. 'You know, the amusements, one-armed bandits, slot machines,' the woman said. 'No,' I answered, 'I don't really know anything about them.'

They both expressed disappointment. They worked in an amusement centre. I had noticed several as I searched Lifford for a place to stay. It was very popular, they both agreed. It would be open the following day and I could go if I wanted to.

The clock on the wall ticked slowly. It was now only a quarter to two and the dance wouldn't be over until two and it would surely be half an hour after that before the owner of the house would get home. I asked about Strabane, just over the bridge in the North, but they said they didn't go there much. Fifteen minutes was then filled with an account by the aunt of a robbery at the amusement centre. We agreed that times were bad, but it was still only five past two.

They talked between themselves for a while, the two of them, while I sat on the sofa immersed in self-pity. I was going to rest for several days, I decided, and in future I was going to walk in small doses. Over the next hour we made several efforts to talk to each other, some of which succeeded to a limited degree. The proprietor finally returned and relieved the aunt and her son at a quarter to four. She found me blankets and opened out the sofa to make a bed.

I fell into a deep sleep, to be woken in the morning by a question: What would I like for my breakfast? I sat up and looked around. It was nine, she said, some of the other lodgers were having breakfast. Did I want mine now? I said I would wait for a while.

It was afternoon when I woke again and the sun was hot. It was time to wash myself, pay the bill and move on.

There was still a festival on in Lifford. A group of boys had brought a huge transistor radio to a piece of grass near the customs post at the bridge. They sat with their shirts off drinking cans of beer, trying to attract the attention of a group of girls who were sitting on the windowledge of a nearby shop and indulging in horseplay. In the main square a man sat on the stage and played traditional Irish tunes on an accordion; people stood and listened.

Around the corner there was a field where there were to be races and games, but most of the children were attracted by a huge empty factory building, with the doors wide open, damp and dark inside with offices near the factory floor. Children were screaming their heads off to hear their voices echo.

The pubs in the town were full, with fellows standing outside, pints in their hands. One pub had sunshades, tables and chairs in a garden with a man playing well-known tunes on an organ: *Yesterday, The Way We Were.* Further up a crowd sat in a run-down bar and listened to a live band play pop songs. I had a few drinks and decided that there wasn't much future in this festival, and left to walk across the border into Strabane.

The army were stopping some of the cars at the checkpoint but they paid no attention to me as I wandered by. There was nothing happening in Strabane. A few kids hung around an amusement arcade; the pubs would remain shut all day as this was the North. The Fir Trees Hotel was at the other end of town.

The woman at reception said they could accommodate me for one night only. The hotel bar was open; it was doing good business.

For the entertainment of guests, the hotel had provided a free copy of a magazine called the *Ulster Tatler*, full of fashion photography, with a column on social life in Belfast by a woman who called herself 'The Malone Ranger' and went to parties on the Malone Road. There wasn't a word about the Anglo-Irish Agreement, signed the previous November by the British and Irish governments, which had increased tension in the North and sparked off a campaign by Protestants with the slogan 'Ulster Says No'. The North according to the *Ulster Tatler* was full of wild parties, nice big houses, good-looking women wearing expensive clothes, and great restaurants. Over the next few months, I was to discover that things were, in fact, rather different from the world depicted in the *Ulster Tatler*.

2

The Hiring Fair

'I saw you before,' I said to the priest.

'When was that?'

'I was at the funeral,' I said. He nodded. I didn't have to explain what funeral, even though it had taken place over a year ago.

'I heard what you said in your sermon,' I said. 'You said it was execution.'

'Yes, that's right.'

*

I was in Strabane. It was the following afternoon. I had called at the priest's house. When he came into the small waiting room, it was like suddenly seeing some familiar face in a new context. It took me a while to remember the context. I realized that over a year ago on a grey day I had watched his face as he stood outside the Catholic church waiting for the third coffin to get through the police blockade.

Three local youths, Michael and David Devine and Charles Breslin, had been shot by the SAS in the early morning as they crossed a field. They were armed, and it was clear that they were either moving armaments or coming from an ambush which had failed. They were shot without warning from high ground. Local people said that they heard them calling out for help, that the SAS had trapped them, trained machine guns on them and opened fire. One hundred and seventy bullets were fired; half of the total hit their targets. No fire was returned.

The youngest of them was sixteen, the oldest twenty-two, two of them were brothers and one had been a snooker champion. The parents of the Devine brothers did not know that their sons were in the IRA. People seemed shocked by what had happened, shocked that these boys whom they all knew had been killed. The local priests issued a statement saying that they believed that the youths could have been intercepted and arrested, saying that they considered the killings to be murder.

The parents of the Devine brothers did not want a military-style IRA funeral for their sons, so there was no difficulty in bringing the two coffins to the church. Charles Breslin, however, was to be given a paramilitary funeral; his coffin was to be draped in the tricolour, his cap and gloves on top, and carried through the streets. The RUC, the police in Northern Ireland, refused to allow this: there was an impasse. The people in the church waited for the third coffin to come.

I remember the greyness of Strabane that day, the low clouds, the light drizzle. I remember that the church bell rang at intervals. I remember the crowd in the housing estate standing around the coffin. I remember the tension, the feeling that the crowd might surge forward against the police.

There were well-known faces among the crowd: Gerry Adams, President of Sinn Fein; Martin McGuinness of Sinn Fein, from Derry; Danny Morrison, Head of Publicity for Sinn Fein. An RUC officer stood apart from the crowd, his face implacable and decisive. His baton was almost three feet long, and made of some thick dark wood. He looked as though he was ready to wait for a long time.

Those who gathered on the street seemed like a group of the dispossessed, their faces were pinched, forlorn, weary. There was a sense of crushing hopelessness about the scene.

After a long time they reached a compromise: the flag could be used but not the cap and gloves. The crowd moved slowly towards the church with the single bell tolling again and again. All along the way they said the Rosary.

The Devine brothers' funeral took place in private in the graveyard on a hill above the town. When it was over army snipers wearing camouflage moved into position in the fields around the graveyard. The paramilitary funeral would have an oration by Gerry Adams, President of Sinn Fein. There was a clear view of the town below, the curling river and the land beyond. The RUC were already waiting for Charles Breslin's funeral to start. They had placed themselves close to the walls that surrounded the cemetery. As soon as the coffin came inside the gates the bearers stopped and the paramilitary cap and gloves were once again put on the coffin.

The coffin was followed by a small pipe band which played Republican tunes. The ceremony was brief as the coffin was lowered, interrupted only by the efforts of the RUC to stop some local youths from sitting on the wall.

The clergy made a hasty exit as Gerry Adams started to speak. He began clearly and factually as though he were reading a news report. 'Last Saturday morning three IRA volunteers were carrying Armalites, bombs and ammunition to a depot when a number of strangers, people who are not from here, do not belong here and have no rights here, murdered them in cold blood, giving them no chance to surrender.'

★

'They're called the Martyrs now,' I said to the priest more than a year later.

'I know,' he said.

I had done a tour of the pubs of Strabane that morning. I had talked to people. Did I know what happened on Saturday? they asked. Did I not know? The Martyrs' Memorial Band tried to go from Strabane to Lifford for a festival and they were stopped by the RUC because they were carrying a tricolour, the Irish flag. The RUC came in with fifty jeeps to stop them.

The band had been set up to commemorate the two Devines and Breslin. They had been trying to go to the same festival as the band I met in St Johnston. Most of them were in their early teens, I was told.

The setting up of a band wasn't the only result of the shooting of the three. Someone had informed, the IRA believed, someone had given information to the security forces, and so they shot a boy called Damien McCrory in Strabane, blaming him for informing.

All the pubs were Catholic pubs; most of the people were Catholic in Strabane. There had been one Protestant pub, which served the security forces, but that had been bombed. The town also had the highest unemployment rate in Western Europe: over fifty per cent of the male adults were officially unemployed. In the 1970s the IRA had blown the town to bits; most shops had suffered. I sat in one pub where there were old photographs on the wall of what Strabane looked like before the IRA campaign: sedate, almost pretty, Victorian.

Some of the gaps had been filled in, but there was nothing Victorian about the place now. There was an overwhelming sense of despair. In the months after the shooting of the Devines and Charles Breslin, the priest assured me, there had been an enormous upsurge in young people joining the IRA. I would have thought that the shooting might have discouraged them, but he said it was the opposite – the anger at what happened drove them in.

Everybody talked about what the RUC and the army were doing. At the end of the summer the Catholic Bishop of Derry would issue a detailed statement about what was going on in Strabane. He would detail accounts of local youths being ordered by the security forces to take their shoes and socks off in the street day after day for no apparent reason. He would detail accounts of petty harassment. Everywhere I went people talked about it.

I was sent to see James Bradley, the former Town Clerk of Strabane, who knew the history of the place, and I found him in a big bright bungalow across the bridge in Strabane. He arranged for me to stay with a family in a nearby estate in a smaller bungalow. I went back to Bradley's several times for tea, to get away from the blight of the town, to try and find out what was going on in Strabane.

On one occasion when I visited him his wife started talking about a relation of hers, the writer and political activist, Peadar O'Donnell and the themes he had dealt with, such as poverty and emigration. Just in passing, she mentioned that her own father had been hired at the Hiring Fair in Strabane. They started to talk about the Hiring Fair, the two of them, as we sat in the kitchen of their house. Her father, Mrs Bradley said, had left home at midnight when he was in his early teens and walked until the morning when he had caught a train to Strabane where he was hired by a Protestant farmer. He had to wait in the town that day until the farmer had conducted his business and then walk behind the farmer's horse as far as Castlederg. He worked there for six months and then he got his wages and was hired again by another farmer.

How quickly we had moved in one generation, from poverty and quasi-feudalism, to this kitchen, the dining area on a different level from the cooking area, a dishwasher, electric washing machine, electric cooker, fridge. But I was still unsure about the Hiring Fair. In the South of Ireland, I had never heard anyone talk of a Hiring Fair, where labourers were hired for six months. I asked them about it again.

James Bradley said he remembered the Hiring Fair in Strabane. I looked at his face, I thought he might be sixty, maybe sixty-five, but no more. How could he remember the Hiring Fair? He insisted. He said that he used to watch them on his way to school, the big farmers, the Protestant farmers from the Lagan valley, the farms on both sides of the Foyle River, where I had walked, and the farmers from around Strabane. He used to watch them feel the boys for muscles, feel their arms to see if they were strong enough. He said they used to think it was funny on their way to school.

They used to gather at the Town Hall, which is now blown up. When did it stop, then, the Hiring Fair? He thought for a while and asked his wife and they puzzled over it. 1938, he said, 1938. It ended just before the war, the war changed everything, there was more work and more money. I told him I had never heard about it before. Everyone in Strabane would remember it, he said, everyone over a certain age.

I went back to my lodging house with something new in my head, beyond the misery of Strabane and the legacy of the Devine brothers and Breslin, beyond the unemployment figures and the complaints about the police, beyond the fact that the IRA had threatened to kill anyone – including council workers – who removed the rubbish from the RUC barracks. Here, down the road here, twice a year, children as young as twelve had come in from the countryside and were rented for six months by people they didn't know, brought to a place they didn't know, and made to work. Those hired were Catholics, and those who hired them were, for the most part, Protestants.

*

I was having breakfast one morning, marvelling at the odour of dog in the kitchen and pondering on how one small dog – noisy, smelly, irritating and fidgety – could cause such trouble in such an otherwise sane and pleasant household. The man of the house kept playing with the dog, exciting the animal, making it jump up and bark, as I was trying to eat my bacon, sausage, egg and toast and drink my tea.

'Do you like dogs?' the woman of the house asked me when her husband and the dog had gone out.

'No, not much,' I said.

We talked for a while, both of us slightly grumpy in the morning, going through things, what I had seen in Strabane, what I thought of it. We had more tea. Her son, she said, was in Long Kesh, serving a long sentence. I hadn't known this; I was surprised. When she heard he had been caught, she said, it was the last thing she expected; she knew he had been involved years before, but she didn't think he was in the IRA any more. Anyway, he was in now, that was where he was. She sighed. We sat there quietly in the kitchen, not saying anything.

Beyond the Bradleys' house was the Leisure Centre, keeping its distance from the bombed-out centre of the town, which had a good swimming pool and sports facilities. The parish of Mellmount had a huge new centre as well, with bars and a big assembly hall, as well as a new school, a new church, and a new priest's house. The playing fields behind the new centre were said to have a drainage system for keeping them dry and useable in winter.

The man behind all this building was Father Mulvey, the parish priest of the Mellmount area of Strabane. He was standing at the door of his house, with a small, suspicious grin on his face, as I came towards him. He invited me in. His housekeeper brought us tea and we talked. What did I think of the divorce referendum which was being hotly debated in the South? I was in favour of it, I told him. We argued about it for a while, whether the power of the church in the South was a good thing: I thought it wasn't, he thought it was. We talked about what difference divorce would actually make in the South.

He had been a curate in Derry for years; he was there for the early Civil Rights marches; he was there for Bloody Sunday. He talked with a bitter amusement about some of the main characters involved. He remembered a moment on Bloody Sunday, after the shooting dead of the thirteen Catholics, when he had seen an officer moving among the soldiers who had been involved, talking hurriedly to each one; he had always believed that a motive was being invented in that moment.

Over the years he had been outspoken against the IRA, and he told me with some relish and a certain amount of drama how he had ejected Martin McGuinness of Sinn Fein from the church grounds when he was canvassing for votes.

However, he had also signed the statement calling the shooting of the Devines and Charles Breslin 'murder'. He wasn't sure about it now, and wondered about the statement's benefit.

Was it possible, I asked him, that the Hiring Fair had continued in Strabane until 1938? Yes, he was pretty sure about it, he nodded. He thought it might have even gone on later. I told him I had never heard of it before. A large number of the women who were hired were raped, he said. He wasn't sure about the exact figure, but it was high.

The housekeeper knocked on the door and told him that James O'Kane was here to see him. James O'Kane was the Independent nationalist Chairman of the District Council in Strabane. He was shown into the room. Here was the Protestant nightmare before my eyes, home rule as Rome rule: the Chairman of the District Council sitting in the house of the parish priest having cosy discussions about what would and would not be allowed. But most of the talk consisted of anecdotes and old stories. More tea was brought. In passing, Father Mulvey asked him if there would be a problem about a bit of land down near the river which the council owned and which the church wanted to use for sports. The Chairman of the District Council told the priest that there would be no problem at all.

*

On my map there was a reference to the Beltany Stone Circle in the Republic, a few miles beyond Lifford. The following day James Bradley drove me there. He said it was hard to find; there were no signposts, but he knew where it was. The sky was grey, but the clouds were high and moving fast with the wind. We drove beyond Raphoe and along a set of narrow roads, inadvertently passing by the turn for the stone circle once and having to double back.

Eventually, we found it and drove up a dirt track to the hill where the stones were. You could see for miles on all sides beyond the small hills to other small hills, some of them still wooded. All of them had been wooded when the stones were placed here first, around 2000 BC. The stones were big and rugged, no attempt had been made to decorate them, embellish them, or sculpt them in any way. They were jagged stones placed in a large circle at the top of this hill. This wasn't art – this was magic.

I started to think about that moment, that second when the final stone was put in place and the circle formed, what difference it would have made to the people who placed it there: something new, powerful, complete. That there was no artifice involved, that they had merely carried them there and made them into a circle gave the stones a greater spirit. I moved around touching them, looking at the land down below. Beltany must have come from *Bealtaine*, the Irish word for the month of May; I said that to James Bradley. 'No, no,' he answered. 'It's even older than that, not *Bealtaine*, but its root, *Baal Tine*, the fire of Baal.' Baal was a Celtic god. *Tine* is the Irish for fire.

We walked down the hill, leaving the stones to their magic, away from the reminder that there was once a time in this place when there were no Catholics or Protestants; the dim past standing there on the crown of the hill, for once a history which could do us no harm, could not teach us, inspire us, remind us, beckon us, embitter us: history locked up in stone.

*

In the days following I asked everyone I met about the Hiring Fair. I wanted to find someone who was hired, who could tell me what it was like, someone who still lived here. Most of those who were hired, I learned, had emigrated to America or to England, as soon as they were old enough. Those who stayed didn't want it known – it was a sort of stigma. There were men who spoke Irish, from an Irish-speaking area, living in Derry and Tyrone; they didn't want anyone to know they spoke Irish, as it would signify that they had come in from Donegal to be hired. I would have trouble finding someone to talk of it.

I was given the name of a town to go to – Drumquin. And the name of a woman – Rose McCullough – by someone who told me he knew her. She might talk, as she had once spoken about it on the radio. I took a taxi to Drumquin and went in search of her, finding her in a housing estate on the edge of the town.

She was in her seventies, a big woman, friendly, open, cheerful. She had talked about being hired on the radio, she said. Could I not find a tape of that? No, I said, I wanted her to tell me herself. She started.

She was thirteen, she said, when she was hired for the first time. It was May. She left the house with her sister and her mother at two in the morning, and walked to Fintown, stopping at another sister's house for tea on the way. They walked in their bare feet with their boots over their shoulders; at Fintown station they put on their boots and caught the train to Strabane at eight in the morning. There were thirty of them altogether. It was six pence from Fintown to Strabane, she remembered, but if you stooped down and pretended you were younger you could travel for four pence.

The train got into Strabane at ten or eleven o'clock in the morning. The farmers were waiting at Strabane station, looking for the best and the strongest, but most of those who wanted to be hired went to the area around the Town Hall, where there was an archway for shelter. 'Are you for hiring, wee cutty?' the farmers would say, and the mother would say yes, because she 'was wild to get us hired', Rose McCullough remembered. The farmer would go through the long list of things he wanted the girl to do: Could she milk, wash, cook, churn? And the mother would answer yes whether she could or not: the money was needed at home.

They were all Protestants, the farmers. The agreement included permission for the girls to go to mass every other Sunday. They were to be paid £5 or £6 at the end of six months.

When Rose was hired, the farmer took her into a coffee shop in Strabane and gave her a mug of cocoa and a big penny bap and took her bundle of clothes, which he kept. He arranged to meet her later at the post office.

'Now wee cutty, you'll have to come with me,' he said to her. She cried, but her mother didn't show any emotion.

She pointed out through the window of the house. 'A place away over there,' she said. That was where he took her. She couldn't read or write. He had left his horse in a stable in Strabane. She remembered him jumping on the horse's back and saying 'you follow me now', and she ran after his horse the three or four miles from Strabane. When they arrived at the house, she was given a cup of tea and a bit of bread. She was given a pile of potatoes. 'You wash those spuds and leave them there until the morning,' he said to her. There was himself, the man who had hired her, and his brother, as well as their old mother in the house. They put her sleeping in a sort of pen at the top of the stairs.

In the morning they woke her at six. It was time for the milking. She had never milked a cow in her life. When she got a bucketful from each cow she thought she was doing well, but when they discovered this they made her go back and get more milk from the cows. They would not give her food on a plate, she said, but they would put a bag on the table and place the food on that. She remembered crying the first day because the milk was sour.

She counted the days, and when November came her time was up. It was like going to heaven, the journey back to Strabane. She thought she was getting home for the winter. But her mother told herself and her sister that there was no money, they would have to go back and be hired again.

She remembered that it was snowing in Strabane that day, and they stood in the street, herself and her sister Annie, and they cried. The second six months was worse. The food was worse. She was caught stealing food and the farmer pulled her around the kitchen by the ear until she threatened him with the bread-knife and he stopped. His son came and made peace. The son wasn't too bad. She was a useless cook; they asked her to make bread one day, but she forgot to put the baking soda in, and the bread had to be fed to the hens.

Every six months she was hired again until she reached the age of nineteen, when she got married. Her husband was hired as well, near Omagh. He came for her on a bicycle and they were married at nine o'clock mass. After the ceremony they went into a nearby house where the woman put bacon and eggs and bread on the table. They walked up to Omagh station and caught the train to Strabane. They spent the day there and then came back to Omagh and, she said, 'he took me on the bar of his bike to my place and he gave me a kiss and a hug and went to his place'.

'There were none of them good,' she said. 'I would go down in one place I was hired to a plantation, and cry, I looked up on to the hill and thought if I could see over the hill I'd see home. I think of the punishment I got – we had to do it or die of hunger.'

Her farmers all paid at the end of the six months, with the exception of one who docked her money for breaking the door of the oven. But there were others who wouldn't pay, one man in particular, who called the police when one of his hired boys took two calves in lieu of payment. He would be watched at the Hiring Fair, but he would always get someone, she said. There was another man who was reputed to have murdered several boys, but no one ever tried to do anything about it.

Did any of them ever molest her? I asked. No, she said, none of the farmers ever touched her but she knew one girl who had twins for a farmer, and had to go home to have the babies. The farmer would have nothing to do with her. 'That was no life, you know,' she said, 'you saw no one's face except old farmers. They were tough times. I know plenty of people around here who wouldn't tell you. They all got the same abuse as I got.'

Most of her brothers and sisters emigrated as most of her parents' family had done before them, as did her own three sons and one daughter. Got out, to England or America. One of her uncles became a millionaire in America.

Her troubles did not stop when she and her husband finally settled down together. He died at the age of thirty-eight, leaving her with five children. She had to go back and work as a farm labourer again. 'They couldn't get enough work out of you,' she said. 'They'd have no pity on you. I don't know what kind of country it was. It was a cruel country.'

She went back recently to the house in Donegal where she was born, where her family still lives. The changes were astonishing: carpets everywhere, rooms built on, a new fireplace, a shower. She marvelled at what the house was like.

'I wish I could spell. I wish I could write a bit myself. You'd nearly call me a liar for telling you what happened. You were just a slave. You never got a day off. You had no money. People wouldn't tell you because they'd be ashamed. I wouldn't be ashamed. I came through it all.'

Her great-granddaughter came in with a friend and they both sat listening to the end of the story. One of Rose's daughters, who is dead now, stayed at home, so she had a family in Drumquin. The two little girls listened carefully to the bit about her not being able to spell. They thought it was funny that an adult couldn't spell. Rose thought it was funny as well, pointing out that she could spell small words, but not big ones like 'wheelbarrow'. The two girls giggled.

When I left Rose I wandered down into the village of Drumquin: I needed a drink. I rang for a taxi and sat at the bar. I told the people in the bar that I had been to see Rose McCullough, and they all started talking in the bar about the Hiring Fair, about who was hired and who wasn't hired. The man beside me said his mother had been hired, but he didn't think his father had been. They pointed to a man at the top of the bar and said he definitely had been hired; they all laughed as they shouted his name down the bar. He looked up in astonishment at all the attention being paid to him.

The taxi driver had more recent events on his mind as we drove back to Strabane. Two of his friends had been taken in by the army at the checkpoint on the bridge to Lifford and told to

strip. When they stripped they were told to put their clothes back
on and they did. They were then told they could go. They
couldn't understand why they had been told to strip. Every bloke
under thirty was being made to take his shoes and socks off by
the army and the police; most of the time the army didn't bother
examining the shoes and socks, he said. Just as in Derry, he said,
there were no discos in Strabane. If you wanted to have a good
time, you went into the Republic. It was good for the taxi trade.

*

The Martyrs' Memorial Band came from a part of Strabane
known as 'Head of the Town' which was a housing estate less
than twenty years old. The sense of depression there was all-
pervasive. Some of the houses were bricked up, others had been
razed to the ground. This was the main breeding-ground for the
IRA in Strabane. A huge mural was painted on one gable end:
'The fools, the fools they have left us our Fenian dead'. The Irish
flag flew high on a mast and its colours, green, white and orange
were also painted on footpaths and gable walls.

*

The afternoon was hot when I took the road to Clady, which
was, like Strabane, right on the border. There were soft clouds in
the sky and other brooding clouds lurking behind them.

My destination was Castlederg.

An army helicopter flew low over the fields and then went
over the town before it turned and flew back out again. I passed
the town dump and the river. I passed along the wall of what
seemed like a run-down estate before I came into Clady, where,
even though I had only walked a few miles, I decided I was due
a drink. There was an Irish flag waving in the housing estate I
passed.

The barman confirmed for me that there was no inn between
Clady and Castlederg and he thought Castlederg was ten miles
away if I went over the hills. I showed him my map, a map which
would cause me immense grief, being an ordinary Michelin road
map of Ireland. He looked at it for a while, shrugged his shoulders
and went back to taking in bets for racing from local youths.

There was an army checkpoint down the hill and beyond it the remains of a public house which still had its name written up clearly: The Smugglers' Inn. Just before the bridge which led into the South was a small filling station, a tiny off-licence and a small shop, handy for those who wanted to avail themselves of the cheaper prices in the North without having also to avail themselves of the army checkpoint. Nip in, get the cheap petrol and nip back out again.

The man who ran the three little businesses between the checkpoint and the border was Billy Flanagan, until recently an SDLP councillor on Strabane District Council, but he had lost his seat to Sinn Fein. He had lost his pub, The Smugglers' Inn, as well, to the IRA.

Bombing was nothing new around here. The bridge at Clady, the same one which still spanned the river Finn, was first blown up in 1688 during the Williamite Wars. Twice this year so far there had been bombs, one in January and one in May. Both had been proxy bombs − the IRA forcing someone at gunpoint to get into a car; then while his family was held hostage, drive with the bomb inside to a certain place, in this case the army checkpoint in Clady, which happened to be opposite The Smugglers' Inn.

The most recent bomb had come at ten past eleven at night. They ran out of the pub and the checkpoint and stood waiting for the bomb to explode. It went off after midnight. Billy Flanagan had added catering facilities for two hundred to the pub, which was blasted to bits. He had closed up after the bomb in January; now, it seemed, he would be closed for good. He was in his early forties, and seemed like someone from whom the gloom never lifted − his shoulders were hunched, the worry fixed in wrinkles on his forehead.

Clady, Flanagan said, was a hundred per cent Catholic. It was free and easy before 1980, when the army began building the checkpoint, believing that the border crossing was being used to smuggle arms. He had stopped serving the army or the RUC in the bar. When the second bomb came the army were in the middle of intensive repair work on the checkpoint. No builder would work for them. The IRA had recently issued a statement which read: 'Our original warning still stands. Anyone who works for the RUC, in whatever capacity, will, once positively identified, be executed.' Over the next few weeks they would execute a few well-known builders.

We wandered through the bombed-out pub. Flanagan's young son came with us. We looked at how all the cans of beer had shrivelled up in the bomb blast. The boy lifted something up and looked at it, studied it for a while, before showing it to his father. 'Daddy,' he said, 'what was that?' His father told him to put it down.

He gave me directions to get to Castlederg over the mountains, warning me that I would go into the South, into the North, into the South again and back into the North. 'How will I know whether I'm in the North or the South?' I said to him. 'You won't know,' he replied, managing a gruff sort of smile.

Within a few months his whole livelihood would be taken away, not just his pub; the petrol station, the shop and off-licence would be purloined by the army, who wanted to extend the checkpoint almost as far as the bridge. They would make him move. People in Strabane would see a thirty-two-vehicle convoy wade through the town in the middle of the night full of supplies for the new army checkpoint at Clady. The compensation would never make up for what was lost.

*

Half a mile up the hill beyond Clady was a different world, made up of different colours, different sorts of houses and fields. The area between Strabane and Clady had been made up of big fields, good land. This, however, was mostly bogland. Fields full of heather, furze, rushes. Soggy, wet fields. The road became narrow as it made its way straight over the hill. The warm day was beginning to fade, but there were a good three or four hours of light left. I saw a rabbit running across a field.

As I wandered higher up this hill, the land became worse; a few sheep grazed morosely among the rushes, a few scrawny trees broke the monotony. I asked a man whom I met to tell me the way to Castlederg. He said I'd be better to go back to Clady, it would be easier to get a lift from there. I said I was walking. He said he still wasn't sure if the road was passable. It used to be, he said, but he wasn't sure if a crater had not been put in the road at the border. He told me where to turn. No one went down there now, he said.

The turn was blocked off with wire, but there was clearly a path across the hills, so I climbed over the wire and made my way along. There was a lone farmer in a tractor in a field. He stopped what he was doing and I could see him watching me. I walked along a dip in the track and up a slight incline towards him. He drove the tractor on to the track and stopped.

'Am I in the North or the South?' I asked him.

'Where are you going?'

'I'm walking to Castlederg. Am I in the North or the South?'

'You're in the North,' he said. 'That's the North there, that dip in the road. That's the South over there where you came.'

I didn't know I had been in the South at all, not since Lifford. I checked my map, but there was no sign of this road on the map.

'You're all right then?' the man on the tractor asked.

'I am,' I said.

Beyond a whole field full of purple heather was a dump, full of broken chairs, plastic bags, tins, bottles and bits of cars. Over the hill were a few farms with long lanes running down to the farm houses. I could hear the sound of gunshot in the distance; somebody was trying to shoot crows, or to scare them away. The road was tarred now, and I enquired from a man who was standing by the door of a cottage whether I was in the North or the South and he said I was now in the South. I told him the route I had taken and asked if it was possible that I had come from the North into the South into the North again and into the South once more without a single signpost or checkpoint, without a significant change in the look of the landscape or the quality of the road.

He laughed. It was possible, yes, sure it was as possible as if I walked two miles ahead I'd be back in the North again, but this time I would meet a checkpoint. It must be a haven for smugglers, I said to him. You could get a grant for an animal in the North and then take it South and sell it, couldn't you? He laughed again, but said nothing.

There was hardly any traffic on the road. The day was still warm and the hard asphalt was starting to hurt my feet. I passed a Garda checkpoint and a Garda looked out at me. I was in the North again, at a fork in the road with no idea which road led to Castlederg. I was just standing there waiting for inspiration when I saw a British soldier peering out of the ditch just a few feet away from me. He was camouflaged, his face blackened; his green and brown uniform blended in with the colours of the fields and the ditch. I saw that he had a few companions wandering around the field with guns pointed straight ahead of them, as though they were looking for something.

Where was I going? asked the soldier. I told him I was making my way into Castlederg. Did he know the way? I asked him. He asked if I was from the South and I said I was. Both roads led to Castlederg, he said. Which was the shorter? He wasn't sure. I decided to go straight on. I saluted him and he nodded cheerfully. One of his companions was sitting in the ditch, plonked down, without any regard for nettles or thistles, with a radio beside him and a large aerial. I greeted him and he said hello.

In the next field there was a thatched cottage which was completely ruined, the thatch had caved in. I could see the other road into Castlederg over to the right. It was milking time now, and fat cows were being led out of the fields towards the milking parlours.

As I passed a small bungalow which was just beside the road, a woman stood at the window with her back to me. There were no curtains on the window and I could see her clearly. As she turned she suddenly caught sight of me from the side of her eye and then with her full vision, she screamed at the top of her voice. I had given her a fright. It was hard to know what to do. It was a lonely road; she probably didn't expect a stranger to pass by like that.

I decided that there was no point in stopping to explain that I didn't mean any harm. Even the idea seemed ridiculous. So I just walked on and when I looked behind, she was there at another window with a few other women, all of them younger than she, all looking at me. I walked on as fast as I could.

On the way into Castlederg I passed an expensive bungalow

with three huge dormer windows which had been built beside a run-down old shack with a galvanized roof. The shack had been abandoned. It was as though the money had come quickly and all together; they had simply built the new house, and when it was ready they had abandoned the old one. The two buildings looked as though they had been set up as a case history for students of social change, so brazenly did they stand there beside each other.

There were more new bungalows on the way down the hill into the town. I went past the church and the RUC station and stopped at the first pub I saw and ordered a pint of beer. There was a stony silence as I came in. The men playing pool continued with their game, and no one spoke.

I was unsure of my ground here. Castlederg I knew, was divided. There were Catholic pubs and Protestant pubs. I wasn't sure which type I was in. I sat there anyway and finished my drink. I had been told there was a hotel here and I asked the barman, who directed me across the road.

As I stood on the street I was approached by an RUC patrol. A very young policeman got out of the front of the car and another out of the back. As the young man asked me for identification, the other one crossed the street and pointed a rifle at me, directly at me, while I rummaged through my rucksack. I was going to ask him if he could ask the other one to put the rifle down, but I didn't want to be taken to the RUC station, or to get involved with the RUC in any way. He told me that he was going to search my bag, and he informed me under what section of some Act of Parliament he was going to do so. I told him that was okay. People came to the window of the pub and were staring out. The policeman across the street still had his rifle trained on me, which I found disturbing. The other fellow began to look through my books, which included Eugene McCabe's *Heritage*; he looked at it for a while: the title story was about a UDR man in Fermanagh meeting his death; I wondered if he knew about it – it had been made into a television play.

'Where are you staying?' he asked.

'In there,' I said, pointing at the building I had been directed to. He helped me put my things back into the rucksack and walked back to the car. His friend with the rifle walked across the road and opened the back door of the car and sat in before it drove away.

'In there' was a luxurious new pub, with a massive video screen. No, the hotel part was shut up, they were doing repairs, the owner said. The only other place I could stay was with a woman across the road who often took people in, the barman told me. When I wandered across to her, she was having building work done as well; she showed me the front room, which was in a state of disarray. No, she couldn't do anything for me. The best place to go would be Strabane.

Strabane seemed years away. It seemed like a week since I had been there, and the idea of going back there was somehow shocking. I went back to the pub and explained my plight to them. A discussion ensued among the men at the bar. Strabane was mentioned again. I said I didn't want to go to Strabane. There was, someone said, a place about eight or nine miles out called The Hunting Lodge, on the road to Omagh. They took in guests. That seemed the best bet, and it was generally agreed that a taxi could be phoned for me to travel out there.

I guessed by the taxi driver's name that he was a Protestant, and as he drove me out towards The Hunting Lodge I asked him if there were pubs in Castlederg he wouldn't go into. These days there were, he said. Things were bitterly divided now. The young people were completely separated into different camps, which had not been the case for their parents. There was a time when Catholics and Protestants lived in a sort of harmony in Castlederg.

He drove along an elaborate network of roads, coming to a crossroads every few miles. There were several ways you could go to The Hunting Lodge, he said, there were so many roads. Most of the roads were quiet, with very few houses. We came to The Hunting Lodge at the end of a long, steep hill with a forest on either side. I paid the taxi driver and he waited to make sure that they had a room to spare. The young woman at the reception desk seemed nervous, and went in search of a very tall older man. They seemed uneasy, but agreed that they had a room free. I waved to the taxi driver and he went off.

All day, since I had passed the army on the road into Castlederg, I had noted an atmosphere of fear, of watchfulness. Even in the bar of The Hunting Lodge – I guessed that the owners and the clients were all Protestants – everyone observed me out of the corner of their eye. No one looked at me straight, no one greeted me. There was a nervous friendliness about the girl who served me my dinner. I felt uncomfortable and, having watched television for a while, I went to bed.

That night I phoned a man called Tommy Kerrigan – a Catholic name if there ever was one – who was a member of Ian Paisley's DUP, a local councillor and, of course, a Protestant. Yes, he would like to talk to me. He arranged that he would come and have breakfast with me the following day. I looked forward to his visit for several reasons, one reason being that he might establish for the people who ran the lodge that I wasn't a threat to them.

It was late morning when he arrived, and we were alone in the dining room. He was a big man, and when I asked him how things were in Castlederg, he had no difficulty knowing where to start. In January Victor Foster, a member of the UDR, local part-time soldiers, was leaving his girlfriend's home and was blown up by an IRA bomb just two hundred yards from his own house. His girlfriend lost an eye; when she came into Castlederg now, she was taunted in the streets.

In April, William Pollock, another UDR man who had moved into a nationalist area, was blown up when he was attaching a trailer to his father's car. William Pollock had been at Foster's funeral, and had remarked to a friend that if anything happened to him he didn't want the top brass of the army or the police at his funeral. Tommy Kerrigan went down to his house the night he was shot; nearly all the parents of all the Protestants who had been shot had turned up to sympathize.

It would take a tear from a stone, he said. 'We see no light at the end of the tunnel, we see nothing, only darkness.' He went through other names, other murders. He emphasized that all the information about the movements of the men who were murdered must have come from locals, neighbours, Catholics who lived nearby. He mentioned a wedding he had been at in 1982; the groom, the bride's sister, the best man and a guest at the wedding were all murdered by the IRA within six months.

'People are just living, wondering who is going to be next, what's the next move, whose funeral is to be the next one,' he said. He continued talking as the girl came to take away the breakfast things.

Just a month previously, the army had come across two armed men and there had been a shoot-out; the men had been able to get away across the border into the Republic. Of the six murders in the Castlederg area over the previous two years, no one had been charged. Nor had anyone been caught for the forty bombings which had devastated the pubs, hotels and business places, as well as the police station in Castlederg. There was, Tommy Kerrigan said, no security.

The IRA were getting more adventurous, he said. They were now using mortar bombs on RUC stations. Recently in Castlederg, they had driven a lorry with a bomb on the back into the grounds of the Catholic church, where there were one hundred children learning Irish inside, and tried to bomb the RUC station across the road.

*

The army was wandering around Castlederg that afternoon in groups of four, rifles at the ready. One of them was walking backwards. I wandered up into a housing estate at the top of the town to see a Sinn Fein councillor, Charlie McHugh. We sat in the front room of his house, drinking more tea.

When he moved into the estate eight years previously, he said, it was mixed, but now the Protestants had moved out. There had been a UDR man and an RUC man living nearby with their families, but they had both left. Most of the Protestants had gone over the past three years.

'There have been a lot of UDR men murdered here,' I said. They were members of an occupying force, he said, even though they were from the area, they were members of the Ulster Defence Regiment, a regiment of the British army. There was a war on. He wouldn't accept the word 'murder'.

We talked for a while longer about the town, how the odd

row broke out between Catholics and Protestants after the pubs shut on a Saturday night, how the odd spate of window-bashing went on, but that the atmosphere in Castlederg was mainly quiet, tense; people walked the streets with their eyes down.

He asked me where I was going next, and I told him I was going to walk into the South again and go on a pilgrimage to Lough Derg. I showed him the sweater I had bought for protection against the notorious cold which came down at night on the island. He told me that the road between Castlederg and the border was one hundred per cent Provo. I would be perfectly safe walking along there, he said.

3

Dark Night of the Soul

I set out the following morning for Lough Derg, having taken a taxi from The Hunting Lodge to Castlederg. It was a beautiful day again, full of hazy sunshine, and beyond Killeter there was a slight breeze. I had no breakfast: the rules for pilgrims to Lough Derg specified that nothing except water was to be taken from the midnight before arrival. Since the twelfth century, Lough Derg had been a site of pilgrimage.

This was Friday morning. All day Friday and all day Saturday I would get nothing to eat on Lough Derg except black tea and dry toast.

Tonight would be a vigil of prayer and fasting. The next time I would sleep would be Saturday night. I would take off my shoes as soon as I arrived, and would not retrieve them until I left the island on Sunday morning. Most of the prayers would be said in the open, even if it was raining. All summer, pilgrims would arrive each day; there was no requirement to give notice.

Two men stopped in a car and offered to give me a lift, but I told them I wanted to walk to Lough Derg. The man in the passenger's seat had done the pilgrimage ten times, he said. He would go later in the summer. It was worse every year, he said. I was lucky, it was my first time, so I didn't know how bad it was going to be. That was the worst thing, he said, suddenly remembering how bad it was going to be.

The driver had never done the pilgrimage. He said he had no bad habits, so he didn't need it. His friend said that the worst part was the long night awake – he never minded the hunger. They wished me luck and drove off.

There were sheep everywhere trying to find sustenance among the rushes, the boggy grass, the bushes, skinny trees, briars and furze. There wasn't a building in sight; it was as though the landscape was tapering out. At night, it would be easy to stray off the road and get lost in the bog – there would be no lights anywhere. If this was Provo territory, as Charlie McHugh had told me, then it was only because no one else could possibly want it. A bungalow appeared with 'Guard Dog' on the gate, and a hundred yards down the road a man was leading a few cows up towards the house. I told him I was going to Lough Derg, and he guaranteed me that I wouldn't see another person between here and there.

A few miles later I had seen nothing of any interest except bundles of turf left out in bright fertilizer bags. I passed by a house on the right-hand side of what was now becoming a track across the hills. There was a car in front of the house, and I was sure that there was a man sitting in it. Up beyond the house there was a tractor blocking the road and a car parked on the edge of the grass. I could see two pairs of legs beneath the tractor, but the frame hid the figures from view. I stopped. Two men seemed to be hiding behind the tractor.

I didn't know what to do. I knew that there was not much history of random killing in the North. Those who were killed were generally selected carefully. So I didn't believe that the two men behind the tractor had a gun pointed at me which they would shoot at any moment, but I did feel that there was something odd about their presence behind the tractor, and the presence of the man in the driver's seat of the car at the house behind me. I stood there for a while. I was going to turn back, retrace my steps into Killeter and find some other way of crossing the border, but I had to be at Lough Derg before three. Otherwise I would have to wait a whole day before going on to the island.

I stood there and shouted at them: 'Hello, hello.' One of them emerged from the shadow of the tractor and peered out at me nonchalantly. I walked towards them only to find that they were mending a part of the tractor, that they had no guns, bombs, or even stones to throw. They greeted me casually and I asked them if the border was far. It was about a mile, they said, and I should have no trouble crossing on foot. I left them, as I had found them, minding their own business.

There was a stream running below the abandoned road I was

now walking on. There were no sheep anywhere, and nothing grew. There were only the damp ridges where the turf had been cut, and the clumps of turf left out to dry in the breeze which was stiffening now. I thought of the turf burning weakly all winter, sending out billows of filthy brown smoke every time the door opened or the wind changed. It looked wet still, as if no amount of wind or sun would take the damp out of it.

Between the turf and the border there was just one abandoned house. I had no trouble spotting the border, which someone had gone to a lot of bother to make impassable. The track was blocked with rusted barbed wire and huge blocks of concrete with rusted iron fenders sticking up from the concrete at all sorts of angles, like a building after a bomb. A few yards away there was a second block of concrete and more iron fenders, and then the bridge over the stream which was also blocked. The bodies of a few abandoned cars lay among all this debris. Even on foot it took a bit of effort to climb over. A motorbike would have considerable difficulty; for a car it would be impossible. The border was blocked.

There wasn't a sound as I passed from the North into the South, except the wind among the trees and the shallow water of the stream rushing through stones. But bit by bit I began to hear the sound of a chainsaw somewhere in the forest which now lined both sides of the road. The road was tarred now and seemed to be in regular use.

Suddenly, I saw Lough Derg. The sky was a light blue and the water was light blue as well, so I had been looking at it for a while before I realized that it was the lake. A few hills came into view between the trees and after a while through a clearing in the forest I could see the green dome of a church and then I could plainly see the island, Station Island. I already knew of the pilgrimage there, from stories people had told me. There is a short story by Sean O'Faolain called *Lovers of the Lake*. There are poems by Patrick Kavanagh and Seamus Heaney about the island as a central repository of the faith of our fathers, Irish Catholicism, where people with simple faith came hoping for a cure or a favour or a strengthening of their belief. They had done this right through the days when Catholic practice was forbidden in the eighteenth century, and despite the specific ban on the pilgrimage in 1704.

It was still a beautiful day. The lake looked wonderful and the island seemed much smaller than I had imagined. I knew it was still before three, so if I walked quickly I would make it before the last boat to the island. I was hungry now, and I dreaded the hunger ahead, the long night's fast. As I moved closer to the island, I grew uneasy. Someone would spot that I was an interloper, a fellow who had not come to pray for a special intention, a person whose dialogue with the Almighty had become somewhat one-sided. I would never be able to bear the hunger, the lack of sleep.

The car park beside the pier where the boats were moored was full of big, shiny cars. I had imagined that the sort of people who came here were poor, from the small farms, from the edges of the towns and cities. One look at the car park put me right on that.

At a kiosk window I paid £10, and discovered that it was not yet two o'clock. I was in plenty of time. I was handed a leaflet which contained the prayers and the timetable for two days on the island, and directed down to the boat.

The boat was almost full, the pilgrims seemed cheerful. They were mostly women, women of all ages, but a few males lurked among them. Jokes were made about the condition we would all be in two days hence when we came off the island. Everyone seemed to have done the pilgrimage before and what they appeared to dread most was rain. They shivered at the thought of rain.

'I hope you brought your woollies,' the woman beside me said. 'Is this your first time?' she asked. I told her it was. She came every year, she said. She felt great after it, even though it was hard, the staying awake was hard.

When a few more pilgrims came the ropes were untied and the boatman steered across Lough Derg to St Patrick's Purgatory on Station Island.

*

The first people we saw seemed to inhabit a different world. They looked cold, their faces were pale and, as they watched us coming towards them, they blinked. They had been starving for two days and they had had no sleep the previous night. They looked exhausted and depressed. Their feet were bare. 'If you knew what was coming you would go back now,' one of them, a woman with a Northern accent, said to a few of us. She laughed. I knew she would get no sleep until ten o'clock that night. I had been reading the timetable. As I walked towards the church, I noticed people huddled up against each other; their expressions seemed even more distressed than those who sat near the water.

In the men's dormitory I put my rucksack down and a woman handed me sheets, which on Sunday morning I was to exchange for the ones already on the bed. The dormitory would be open between seven and eight, and I could lie down for a while then, she said, but it would be closed all night for the vigil.

I looked through the leaflet, which said that pilgrims had to begin the stations on the first day and complete three before twenty past nine. I went out and began.

'Begin the Station with a visit to the Blessed Sacrament in St Patrick's Basilica,' the leaflet said.

'Then go to St Patrick's Cross, near the Basilica, kneel, and say one Our Father, one Hail Mary and one Creed. Kiss the Cross.'

St Patrick's Cross was a small, iron structure. Pilgrims were already kneeling there, some of whom had rosary beads in their hands, all of whom had a look of intense concentration on their faces as their lips moved in prayer. I knelt beside them. The Creed was the Apostles' Creed and was written out for those who didn't know it.

As each person finished the prayers they approached the Cross and put their lips against the cold metal. There was a deep silence in the area in front of the church and the atmosphere of reverence was unbroken by the new arrivals from the boat.

'Go to St Brigid's Cross, on the outside wall of the Basilica,' the leaflet now directed. 'Kneel and say three Our Fathers, three Hail Marys and one Creed. Stand with your back to the Cross, and, with arms outstretched, renounce three times the World, the Flesh and the Devil.'

I kissed the Cross and continued to the next station and knelt down. Silently, the prayers were said again, and then each of my companions rose to their feet and stood with their back to the wall, stared straight ahead and stretched out both arms saying quietly: 'I renounce the World, the Flesh and the Devil.' Each of them did this three times, without the slightest trace of embarrassment, and I followed suit, saying the words as well.

'Walk slowly,' the leaflet then instructed, 'by your right hand, four times around the Basilica, while praying silently seven decades of the Rosary and one Creed at the end.'

The pilgrims who had not slept sat around the back wall of the Basilica. There was a strange lifelessness about them; they seemed not to take much interest in what was happening around them. Behind the Basilica was a wall built right against the lake water; the water was clean and unruffled. I looked over at the low hills across the lake, the soft, muted colours in the afternoon heat. I walked around the Basilica, trying to keep pace with the people I had knelt down beside at the beginning. I didn't pray, and tried instead to empty my mind, not to dwell on anything in particular, to keep my concentration fixed on nothing, to enjoy being here among complete strangers.

'Go to the penitential cell or "Bed" called St Brigid's Bed (the one nearest to the bell tower), but if there is a queue take care to join it before going to the Bed,' the leaflet said.

There was no queue. The beds, or the cells, were low circular brick walls with a cross in the centre and enough space to move around or kneel between the wall and the cross.

'At the bed,' the leaflet instructed, '(a) walk three times around the outside, by your right hand, while saying three Our Fathers, three Hail Marys and one Creed; (b) kneel at the entrance to the Bed and repeat these prayers; (c) walk three times around the inside and say these prayers again; (d) kneel at the Cross in the centre and say these prayers for the fourth time.'

I followed the group and began to make my way around the outside of the bed. I didn't find the bare feet part of the penance difficult or painful, but the constant kneeling on stone was becoming difficult – my knees were getting sore.

There was privacy about each pilgrim's prayer, although the movement around the beds was communal and public. Each face was set in an expression of deep, personal ritual, which made it easy to understand why no photographers were allowed on the island.

So odd and intense indeed, so private and unashamed was the atmosphere, that a group of young people began to laugh nervously. Nobody paid any attention to them. Their laughter wasn't mocking, and they did not intend to sneer at those who were praying. They tried to stop themselves and as they did their laughter grew louder and slightly hysterical. They knelt at the bed, waiting for the laughter to stop, their heads bowed, their bodies shaking in mirth, as the pilgrims moved around the beds.

Having followed the instructions of the leaflet once, I discovered that the entire process had to be repeated three more times on the way around three identical beds: St Brendan's Bed, St Catherine's Bed, St Columba's Bed. People moved with a slow, quiet zeal as though they were working in a field, kneeling down and standing up again, moving around a small piece of ground before kneeling once more. All this ritual just added up to one Station. It was going to have to be repeated nine times before I got off the island, and the first one hadn't even finished yet.

The heat of the afternoon was beginning to fade, although it was still warm. I continued on the Station, even though I had begun to find the elaborate instructions of the leaflet irritating and the ritual of the kneeling, rising, praying and walking around meaningless. But the first Station still hadn't ended.

'Go to the water's edge; stand,' said the leaflet. 'Say five Our Fathers, five Hail Marys and one Creed. Kneel and repeat these prayers.'

I became interested again as I stood there with my hands joined and my back to the pilgrims who were moving among the beds, kneeling, standing up, moving around again like ants in an anthill. Here I stood and looked across the lake, the small waves of lake water furrowing up against the stones. I was hungry, I was tired, I was bored. But there was something wonderful in the poetry of this, hundreds of people moving on a small piece of ground, quietly praying and coming then to the edge of the water to stare towards the shore and pray.

I stayed longer than the others, just looking, idling, until I glanced down at the leaflet again to find that there was more: 'Return to St Patrick's Cross, kneel and say one Our Father, one Hail Mary and one Creed. Conclude the Station in the Basilica by saying five Our Fathers, five Hail Marys and one Creed for the Pope's intentions.'

I couldn't take any more. I had done enough. I carefully slipped out of the stream of pilgrims, made sure that no one noticed I had scrapped the last two sections of the Station, and sat down in the sunshine against a wall. I felt depressed now, having been elated a few moments ago as I stared at the water. I didn't know how I was going to get through the next two days. It was only four o'clock. Mass was at six-thirty, night prayers and benediction at nine-thirty and then there would be prayers all night and all the next day. I walked down as far as the pier and wondered if I shouldn't just get my bag and go. I could make the border town of Pettigoe before dark, maybe even get on a bit further, have a meal, a few drinks, a long night's sleep. I had seen the island. I knew what it was like.

I thought about this as I made my way to the tea room for the only meal of the day. There was a choice between tea and coffee; coffee seemed to be the only innovation introduced to the island since the fourteenth century. There were hard little buns – completely tasteless – like flat stones; there was dry toast; and to wash this feast down I asked for black tea. There was no restriction on the amount consumed. The woman beside me at the table advised me to eat as much as I could – there was a long night ahead. There was a big crowd, she said; she had heard that five hundred people came over from the mainland before three o'clock, and were here until Sunday.

The tea was strong and hot. I ordered cup after cup, long after I had given up the rock buns, and tried to eat the dry toast. I had visions of the buns and the toast rolling themselves into a hard ball at the bottom of my stomach and sticking there all weekend. I finished up, realizing that this would be my last meal for twenty-four hours.

I discovered when I went outside and took a walk around the small island that the pilgrims were mostly women, but there were fellows my own age as well as older men. I discovered, too, that you could read anything you liked. One man had Seamus Heaney's *Station Island*; another had Lee Iacocca's book on his life and times in big business. But the most important thing I discovered was that you could talk: there was no rule of silence; those who prayed did so in the manner prescribed by the leaflet, or in the Basilica. The rest of the time was spent talking. It was easy to begin a conversation. Every time I sat down beside someone they asked me where I was from, and was this my first time.

A good few minutes could be filled with these two subjects. I discovered that most of them were from the west and the north-west of the country: Mayo, Roscommon, Leitrim, Longford, Derry, Donegal, Sligo. Everyone took the same line on the quality of the suffering. The hunger wasn't too bad, the bare feet weren't really a problem, it was the staying awake, the long night of vigil that would break your heart.

At half past six we all crowded into the church for evening mass. There were almost a thousand of us, half of whom had come the previous day and would soon be going to bed. After mass I went up to the dormitory and lay on my bunk bed. The chap who had staked a claim to the bed below had removed his bag and left no trace. He did not reappear, and I concluded that he had decided to return to the mainland.

Night Prayer was followed by Benediction. I had always loved Benediction. I knew the hymns in Latin, so this was a great opportunity to participate totally in the pilgrimage by singing *O Salutaris Hostia* in a loud voice. The smell of incense filled the church, and we bowed our heads when the monstrance was raised.

It was almost dark now and the full moon rose in the sky. The air was thick with midges: it was going to be a hot night. The water was calm on the lake. It would make all the difference, the hot night, a woman told me; there was nothing more miserable than a cold wet night for the vigil.

At ten-fifteen the doors were closed and the vigil began. There was a bat flitting around in the upper reaches of the Basilica now, sometimes swooping down low, to the consternation of those in the church. The priest began by asking the pilgrims what they did when weeds grew in their garden, did they just cut the tops off the weeds, asked the priest? Did they ignore them, let them grow, leave them there? Or did they pluck them by the roots, dig down deep to eradicate the weeds? The congregation sat in obedient silence.

I looked up at the bat; the movements helped to keep my mind off the sermon, which went on to compare the garden with the weeds to the soul with sin. What do you do with sin, the priest wanted to know? Do you ignore it, let it fester, add to it? Or did you ask God's forgiveness in true sorrow? He implored us, at the beginning of our vigil, to take the latter course. He told us as well that if we were found that night or the following day to be lying down or stretching out, we would be told to get up.

The sermon was followed by the Rosary, and after the Rosary the doors were opened and the four Stations began. We stayed in the church, and the moving from Bed to Bed was done in our imagination. We moved around the church, pretending that we were outside among the Beds. We stood up, moved around, knelt down, saying the prayers in unison. We weaved around each other, walking up the stairs to the balcony, coming down the stairs, moving over to the other balcony, walking around the church, kneeling down on the bare ground, or on pews. All five hundred of us began to pray all night, with the lake water and the full moon just outside the door, and the bat high up in the church. I had done just one Station that day, which I had found impossible to finish; everyone else had done three. The fourth began at twelve-thirty, the fifth at two o'clock, the sixth and seventh were scheduled for three-thirty and five o'clock in the morning.

The first two were unbearably long, and no amount of movement around the inside of the church, or trips into the open air, relieved the sheer monotony. I began to join in the prayer as a way of getting through the night. This wasn't St Patrick's Purgatory, this was hell. At three in the morning it seemed to have been going on for an eternity. The night wore on slowly, each part of the Station seemed longer than the last one. I was hungry and I was tired. Even the dawn lacked interest, no huge drama in the sky, or sudden appearance of the sun, just a dull greyness emerging.

In between Stations there was a break and we all crowded into a room which jutted right out on to the lake, but otherwise resembled a waiting room in a train station. Everybody talked. How was it going? they wanted to know. The next few hours are the worst, everyone said. If you can get through the next few hours, you'll be all right. Everyone was gentle when they spoke; there seemed to be a kindness building up between us.

At six-thirty there was a mass. It was hard now to stay awake, since there were no movement and no loud prayers. Those who had slept all night and were to depart that morning looked like a separate breed. The Prior said mass, and several times during the ceremony he clapped his hands and ordered the congregation to stand up so that those sleeping could be isolated and encouraged to wake up. Sometimes it took people a while to realize where they were as they woke up in the church.

The sermon was less gentle than that of the night before, although equally free in its metaphors. The famine in Ethiopia, the Prior said, had been caused by deforestation, which had been caused by drought. Here in Ireland, we knew what famine was like, but now, thank God, we could feed our people. But we had drought of a different sort: a moral drought – which would eventually cause the decline of religious practice. This involved in particular the decline in the importance of family life, and the sanctity of marriage, he said, and it was our duty to stop this drought. The Prior didn't need to mention that the divorce referendum would take place in the Republic the following Thursday: everyone understood. The opinion polls were still saying that the Church was fighting a losing battle against the introduction of divorce; this was a crucial weekend in the campaign.

Mass was to be followed by confession, which, he said, was particularly important for those doing the pilgrimage. He made it clear that confession would be well organized, so that everyone in the church would just leave their seats and walk up to the altar rails. I now had a problem. Praying was one thing, and singing hymns was fine, but telling my sins to a priest was something I hadn't done since I was fifteen. There would be no escaping once I was in the church. I was going to have to stay out during the break and hide. Otherwise, I was going to have to start remembering all my sins.

I sat in the waiting room during confession, cunningly called Sacrament of Reconciliation in the leaflet, despite the efforts of two priests to remind me that confessions were being heard. After a while I sneaked up to the dormitory where the others were getting ready to depart. It struck me like a thunderbolt that there was nothing stopping me walking off with them. Even if somebody noticed, I could just declare frankly that I had had enough. I stood at the window and looked out at the clear blue sky over the lake.

It was still only nine o'clock, and the first boat would not depart for an hour. I had time to brood over my plight. I could book into the hotel in Pettigoe, have a large breakfast, read the morning newspapers, get into bed, listen to the radio for a while and then fall into a deep and well-deserved sleep.

The sun was hot now, and it was going to be a sweltering day on the island. It was that, rather than duty, which made me stay. I thought it might be okay if I lay around in the sun, while the others prayed, if I read a book at the water's edge while the hot sun beat down. Time moved slowly all morning, however; at twelve o'clock I went and renewed my Baptismal Promises, which involved renouncing the devil, which I was glad to do. Afterwards, I went into the dining room and devoured dry toast as though it were caviar, and black tea as though it were vintage champagne. Everyone said that they were tired and would sleep well when this was over; a woman asked me how many Stations I had done and I told her I had a few to do still, hoping she didn't know that I hadn't completed any.

Boatloads of pilgrims began to arrive fresh from the mainland, looking pleased with themselves. This was a sign that our ordeal was coming to an end. I felt terrible. The tiredness was growing and with the tiredness an intense consideration of time. It was three o'clock now, so there were seven more hours left before bedtime, so it would be like the period between six in the morning and now, which was also seven hours and which had been an unconscionably long time. I decided that another Station, if taken seriously, would fill at least an hour, and keep my mind on something other than the number of hours between now and sleep.

Evening mass was at six-thirty and afterwards I went up to the
dormitory and lay on my upper bunk. A few cubicles away, a
number of youths were having a loud conversation which centred
on food. What would they eat when they went home the next
day, they asked each other. They would have to wait until after
midnight, as the rules insisted, and then, one said, he would start
with five new potatoes with gravy, two burgers, rashers, sausages
and beans. The others added to the list: chips were mentioned,
as well as peas, chops, steak, onions and mushrooms. Down below
the new pilgrims were making their way through the Beds.

Every hour had been carefully counted and noted as it went
by. All I wanted was sleep. After night prayer and Benediction, I
went straight to the dormitory. The two men in the opposite
bunk were friends, they were in their late fifties. We wished each
other goodnight.

'You'll feel great in the morning,' one of them said to me. I
told him I was too tired to sleep. 'You'll sleep all right,' he said
to me. Soon there was silence in the dormitory, and outside the
summer's night was coming down slowly. I fell asleep.

When I woke in the morning I could hear them whispering
to each other. 'Mike,' one of them said, 'Mike.' He repeated it a
few times. I was wide awake, comfortable in the bed. There was
a hint of morning light coming through the window.

'Mike, what time is it?' he asked.

'It's half five,' the other answered.

I felt elated; I felt a sense of wellbeing. I was ready for the
bell to ring at six, ready to get up in time for morning mass and
prayer.

* * *

I had been warned the previous day to be on my guard at the
end of mass. There was one more Station to be done and a long
queue would develop; it was important to be at the head of
that queue. The first to finish the last Station were also first on
to the departing boats. Get near the door of the Basilica, I was
told, and move sharply as soon as mass is over.

Others had the same idea, and scrambled with equal haste
towards the door to begin the Station. This involved moving

through the first few Beds and then around the Basilica, while saying seven decades of the Rosary at breakneck speed. I was enjoying the morning, with the glint of the sunlight on the lake and the prospect of getting off the island.

I didn't say a single prayer, but I knew that my companions could never have said seven decades of the Rosary in the time they spent trotting around the Basilica to the bottleneck at the entrance to St Brigid's Bed, where a clerical student was placed to control the queue. They cheated, most of them, to the considerable annoyance of those who kept the rules, who said the seven decades of the Rosary in an orderly fashion and so ended up at the end of a long queue.

I went into the men's hostel and washed my feet lovingly in hot water, letting them soak at some length. All around me groans of satisfaction could be heard from other pilgrims who would soon put on their shoes. I gathered up my rucksack, and went outside to join the eager queue for the first boat. I talked for some time to a middle-aged woman from Derry about the divorce referendum, and we both agreed that it would be wonderful if it were passed, despite the sermon we had listened to on the subject.

Soon the sermonizer himself, the Prior of Lough Derg, Monsignor Gerard McSorley, arrived. He was a changed man. He was in great form, laughing and joking. He blessed us as we got into the boat and we waved at him cheerfully as the boat made for the shore.

I set off walking again, towards the village of Pettigoe, but I had hardly gone a hundred yards when a car stopped. A man I had met on the island pulled down the window and offered me a lift. There was a nun in the back of the car.

'Where are you going?' I asked him.

'Dublin,' he said. I didn't want to go to Dublin.

'Are you going through Enniskillen?' I asked.

He checked his map and said that he was. I got into the front seat and he introduced me to the nun, his sister. He told me he was a priest. Both of them told me that they thought the pilgrimage had done them good, and I said I thought it had done me good as well.

They dropped me in the real world, in front of the Railway

Hotel in Enniskillen. It was a Sunday morning, almost midday. I bought the newspapers and sat myself down in the Railway Hotel with a pint of Lucozade, soft drinks being permitted on the last day of the pilgrimage, but nothing else until midnight except black tea and dry toast. The Lough Derg spell was broken, however, and the age-old system of self-mortification meant nothing now. I didn't feel even slightly guilty as I sat among the Sunday drinkers and ordered chicken sandwiches. I devoured them when they came and when I had finished them I ordered more. After a while, I asked for the lunch menu and got through an enormous lunch in the dining room: soup, roast beef, mashed potatoes, chips, carrots, cauliflower, fresh fruit salad and coffee. The pilgrimage was over.

4

A Boat Trip on Lough Erne

The result of the divorce referendum was made known the following Friday morning. It was clear and overwhelming: the country had voted no. I was in Monaghan, at Annaghmakerrig, the house which Sir Tyrone Guthrie had left to the Irish nation as a retreat for artists. I was about to take a boat trip on Lough Erne with Bernard Loughlin, the director of the Tyrone Guthrie Centre, his wife Mary and their two children, Maeve and Eoin.

Guthrie's house was a modest manse rather than a huge mansion. The front windows looked on to a lake with a hill on the other side. Guthrie's presence was everywhere in the house: the books in each room were his books, with inscriptions from colleagues and friends. Along the corridor upstairs was a big board with photographs of his productions, newspaper cuttings about his work, magazine articles about his achievement as a director. He specified in his will, when leaving his house to the nation, that the artists should eat together in the evening. The house was supported by the Arts Councils, North and South; people came from both sides of the border. The area around the house was still a mixed society, with thriving Church of Ireland, Presbyterian and Catholic congregations.

We drove to Enniskillen. A few days earlier I had gone back to Dublin to register my vote, as the opinion polls began to swing away from a 'yes' result. 'A woman voting for divorce is like a turkey voting for Christmas,' had become the slogan. What would abandoned women and children live on? was the constant cry. The majority had voted to keep the ban on divorce in the Irish Constitution.

We stocked up with food and drink in Enniskillen and drove to Kesh, where our boat was waiting for us. Lough Erne was navigable as far west as Belleek, and as far east as Belturbet.

A white heat had descended on the lake, humid and thundery as we moved off. Everything in the distance was shrouded and filtered by this calm light. Cormorants were diving for fish. As we travelled between the shore and the small islands the day began to improve, the vague white sky clearing noticeably to blue, and the heat intensifying. The lake was deserted. A lone heron sat on a rock. We passed by Crevinishaughy Island, steering by the principles laid down: that the boat must go on the white side of the white and red markers. The islands and the shore were lined with trees. We had the roof of the dining room on the boat pulled back. The only sound was the boat's engine, the cry of the odd bird, and babble of the children as we approached White Island.

We tied the boat up at the jetty, and walked up to the ruins of the church, which had a rare Hiberno-Romanesque doorway. Inside the ruin, however, and under a sort of stone shelter built out from the north wall, was something more interesting. Eight figures, found on the island at various times, dating from the ninth, tenth or eleventh centuries, were cemented on to a stone wall. It was clear that some of the figures were related, and made by the same hands, but others stood apart, were much smaller, seeming to serve a different purpose. It was like looking at passengers on a train, placed beside each other for no good reason.

Seven of the faces were still plain, most of them wore a somewhat disgruntled expression. One of them, the last in the series, which was just a stone head stuck into the wall, looked positively unhappy. The two largest figures carried with them something of the pomp of the Church, their bells and croziers carved into the stone with great clarity. They had been found among the stones on the island; here they seemed oddly sanitized in the way they had been preserved; they seemed to be joining the rest of the population, North and South, in saying 'No'. Their mouths on the word for eternity. 'No. No. No.' 'Ulster says No.' 'The Republic says No.' The first figure, however, looked as though she could survive in any environment. She would stand out in any company. Her hands, it should be said, were not by her side. They were down between her legs, displaying her pudenda. She had a fixed grin on her face, which seemed to express the joys of lust, she was egging you on, her face full of temptation, her cheeks bulging: she had no shame. 'Yes,' she was saying, 'yes, yes, yes.'

Officially, she was called a *síle-na-gig*, and statues akin to the one on White Island had been found in other places in Ireland and England. But here on White Island, because of her sharing the same four walls with these seven clerics and malcontents, her representation of freedom, fun and sexual frolics as well as fertility and the lure of lust was more emphatic. We had a great time looking at her, discussing her, putting words in her mouth as well as taunting the poor clerics stuck there in stone, unable to answer back.

On the boat again, we doubled back towards Belleek, half of which was in the South, strengthened by our encounter with early Christian Ireland.

In Enniskillen I had bought a bottle of champagne, which was now cool enough to drink. We filled our glasses with champagne as we moved west towards Belleek. I proposed a toast to 'The Plain People of Ireland' for their wisdom in deciding that we, in the Republic, would have no divorce. We drank to that. We drank, as well, to the Catholic bishops of Ireland, who had encouraged the people to vote no, and to various politicians for making their views so well known. We drank to them as the blue sky gave way once more to a white haze. We drank, finally, to the *síle-na-gig* on White Island until all the champagne was gone and it was time to prepare dinner.

We weren't sure whether we were in the North or the South, so after dinner we set out to investigate which State we were in, and to find out where the shouting and cheering which we had heard while eating dinner had been coming from. The first problem seemed almost insoluble. It seemed we were in the North when we were having our dinner, but on our way to Belleek we wandered momentarily into the South, and as we passed into the town itself we were back in the North. The factory, which produced Belleek china and pottery, we discovered was in the North; it was on the northern side of the bridge.

There was a festival on, we were told, the pubs would be open late and the noise we had heard was the parade, which was now over. We took a walk up and down the town and went into a pub, where we were promised music, organized by the Arts Council of Northern Ireland. There was no music, except the snores of a fellow who had fallen asleep at the counter and was being left undisturbed. After a feed of orange and crisps the children were brought back to the boat by their parents, while I crossed the border into the South to the Border Inn to sample the beer at well over £1 a pint. Despite the high prices, the Border Inn was doing good business. It was much more comfortable than any of the pubs in Belleek, or at least the part of Belleek which was in the North, and it was already showing a videotape on a huge screen of the parade which had just occurred. This was what the southern pub had to do to attract customers.

The clientele stood watching themselves in fascination as they had appeared in fancy dress not long before. They roared out as they saw neighbours and friends on the back of lorries which had taken part in the parade, but as closing time approached at eleven-thirty, everybody had to drink up and the video screen was turned off. For further drinking it was necessary to return across the border.

*

The sun was hot the next morning, hotter even than it had been on Lough Derg, but there was still a haze around the horizon and a white edge to the heat which spelled out thunder. We had booked into a fancy restaurant for our dinner in the village of Ballinaleck, which was way up the lake, beyond Enniskillen, so we had a long day's travelling to do.

We moved east, retracing yesterday's journey, passing White Island, where our *síle-na-gig* displayed her wares to the four winds. An army helicopter came towards us, flying lower and lower as it approached the boat until it was right over our heads, before moving off in search of some other prey. The wide lake was almost deserted; a few other pleasure boats and the odd fishing boat came and went, but mostly there was just us.

All the islands were used by the early Christian settlers, and there was an exquisite plainness about the high cross they had built at Inishmacsaint; there was no ornament, etching or design on the stone. The cross dated from the eighth or ninth century, and stood beyond the church. It was high, maybe twelve or fourteen feet, imposing, exuding a powerful, grey solidity. I stared at it. According to ancient legend – as quoted in Mary Rogers' *Prospect of Fermanagh* – it rotates three times as the sun rises every Easter Sunday.

We started up the boat again, and went towards Enniskillen, passing by Portora Royal School where Oscar Wilde and Samuel Beckett were educated. Beckett wrote in *The Unnamable*: 'They gave me courses on love, on intelligence, most precious, most precious. They also taught me to count, and even to reason. Some of this rubbish has come in handy on occasions, I don't deny it, on occasions which would never have arisen if they had left me in peace. I use it still, to scratch my arse with.' We passed by the police station recently mortar-bombed by the IRA.

We moored the boat at Enniskillen, beside the big new leisure centre, and found a chip shop for the children, gave them money and sent them in. We then walked deliberately down the main street. Our destination was William Blake's pub, the finest public house in Ireland, North or South. The wooden ceiling was high and the bar was lit by bright lamps; there was nothing of the *shebeen* about this place, no sense of drinkers huddled together in a half-lit room, full of smoke and stale smells. This was a cathedral of a public house, opulent, confident and beautiful. Just as whiskey matures in wood, there was a feeling that the air in the pub, enclosed as it was by the wooden ceiling, walls and floors, had been maturing as well and improving the state of the drinkers.

Afterwards it began to rain. The thunder raged all night, or so I'm told. The boat rocked, there was lightning in the sky, the rain poured down, but I heard not a single sound. I slept until morning, when the children decided that it was time we were awake, and came down to disturb us.

It was raining still, so there would be no swimming today. We were tired, irritable and slightly hungover. I was suffering from mild sunburn. There would be no point in cruising along in the rain. We had no idea what to do. What do you do in a boat on a rainy day with three hungover adults and two energetic children? We went back to Enniskillen, past the fishermen's shacks at the

Killyhevlin Hotel, past the castellated, ivy-covered house on the banks of the river with its own jetty, past the new theatre.

The streets of Enniskillen were like the streets of some ghost town, which had been hit by the plague, or terrorized by a fearsome cowboy. No one was in the main street at eleven-thirty in the morning. None of the shops was open; the purchase of newspapers involved a long journey up the town. Needless to say, the pubs were closed. The Royal Hotel was open, however, and we ventured in, looking for coffee. There was no one in the hotel. We went looking for someone to operate the coffee machine in the coffee shop upstairs. We found, instead, a small prayer meeting in session in a back room of the hotel being run by a sect which had no church of its own. We were careful not to disturb them.

When we finally made our way back to the street, having been served our coffee, there were lines of grim-faced church-goers moving towards the Protestant church. They were impeccably dressed, solid citizens of Enniskillen, eager for prayer and hymn-singing on Sunday morning. We were scruffy and unhappy at the prospect of a dull Sunday holed up in a boat. There was no future for us in Enniskillen; we needed to get moving, so we faced the boat east in the direction of Bellinaleck and aimed for Knockninny.

Dinner was eaten without much relish when we got to Knockninny; nobody had much to say, the papers were uninteresting and were now to be found in wrinkled sections in all parts of the boat. The water outside was like thick, cold soup, but the sky was brightening and the rain had stopped. A few other boats were moored to the jetty. We decided to walk to Derrylin, a few miles away. We had hopes of a hotel there, where we could drink. I had come to the conclusion that drink was the only thing which would revive me. We walked along the narrow road as the rooks and jackdaws created havoc in the trees, passing by a small, low Methodist church with some of the congregation, a few men and boys, standing outside chatting, their hands in their pockets. Bernard told me then about a priest from Derrylin who was writing a book and had come to work at the Tyrone Guthrie Centre. The priest lived just opposite the scene of the killing of the third Graham brother. All three brothers had been in the

UDR, and all three were killed by the IRA. The third one worked as a bus driver, and was collecting the children from the Catholic school to take them to Enniskillen to the swimming pool when they shot him. As we walked into the village, Bernard told me how the killers had roared as they escaped in a van, let out war whoops, cries of joy and bravado. The priest had come out of his house at the sound of the shots. He had heard them and seen two men escape.

*

The street in Derrylin was lined with cars. Something was stirring. We smelled a hotel. Drink. We walked past the filling station to the hotel. The doors were open and room after room was full of drinkers. The Gaelic Athletic Association, God bless it, was having a fund-raising dance and drinking session that night. The bar would be open until two. But we left around midnight, having had our fill, and went back through the dark to the jetty at Knockninny.

We sat on the roof of the boat and talked quietly. The steel-grey water was totally calm, disturbed by nothing but the odd splash of a bird. The quiet was disrupted only by bird call, wings hitting against water. Sometimes, we stopped talking and just listened to the night.

The islands in front of us were black against the grey. Each one had been inhabited by the monks. The name Knockninny came from Cnoc Ninnidh, the hill of Saint Ninnidh, who had also founded the monastery at Inishmacsaint in AD 530. He is said to have fasted during Lent on the hill above the lake at Knockninny.

The night was clear with each sound from the water, with each fish turning over in its sleep, it seemed that there was life close by, something moving. It would have looked exactly the same, with maybe a few more trees, when the monks were rowing from island to island in the seventh century. Some of the islands had been inhabited then, as a few still were now.

It rained all day the next day, the children grew more cranky, the windows steamed up. This was the last day of the cruise, and we made our way back to Kesh with a brief stop at the new theatre in Enniskillen, where we had coffee and a breath of fresh air. The lake, which had been dazzling with sun on Saturday, was now grey and dirty-looking. I was glad to kiss the children goodbye and go on my way, while the rest of them drove back to Monaghan.

5

Facing the Music

I came to the small Fermanagh village of Ballinamallard for the
Twelfth of July, and booked into the local hotel. It wasn't long
after midnight when I was awakened by sounds beneath the
window. 'Fuck the Pope!' said a voice.

Ballinamallard was neat that day. It had been festooned in red,
white and blue flags and bunting. Barns and haysheds had been
taken over, and were full of long tables with white tablecloths set
out for teas and suppers. A huge box of sausages had arrived at
the hotel – enough to feed an army. Loaves of brown bread came
too. This was 'history in the making', a man told us. This was
the first time County Fermanagh had held its Twelfth of July
Orange Parade in Ballinamallard. Tomorrow would be a great day
for the town.

The television news was full of ominous stories about the
Twelfth, how marchers were insisting on going through the Catholic housing estates in Portadown, how elsewhere tension was
high because of Protestant feeling about the Anglo-Irish Agreement. No one on any of the bulletins on BBC or RTE mentioned
Ballinamallard; there was no problem here, no problem about
Catholic housing estates, nor Catholic sensitivities. There were
simply no Catholics in Ballinamallard.

*

'Fuck the Pope!' the voice beneath the window repeated. The
man below the window had been drinking. Since the trip on
Lough Erne I had been in Enniskillen for some time now,
drinking in Blake's, swimming in the public baths, and exerting
myself as little as possible. I hadn't walked an inch, let alone a
mile. Soon I would start walking again, but not yet, O Lord, not
yet. Now I was in bed wondering if the man below the window

had any idea that up above him was a papist from Wexford. Eventually, having made his point, he went home.

The following morning there were signs up everywhere advertising Meat and Plain Teas. Outside the bus station a brigade from the Salvation Army were trying to save men's souls. Members of the RUC were wandering about, joking with the residents of Ballinamallard, whose big day it was. The bands would march from a field on the Enniskillen side of the town to the other side, march back, and then return to their buses and go home. When they got home, they would march up and down the main street of their town, as they had done this morning, before dispersing.

Each band had a beautiful banner, with the name of its place of origin clearly marked and a scene from the pageantry of Unionism and Orangeism painted on to the cloth. They came from places with Gaelic names: Clabby, Meenagleragh, Mullaghboy, Cornafanog, Glasmullagh, Augharegh; from places with English names: Florencecourt, Castlearchdale, Scotshouse, Brookeborough, Maguiresbridge, Church Hill. Some of the men carried swords, some wore bowler hats, most wore sashes, they played pipes, they beat drums, they played whistles and flutes, they beat more drums, they played accordions. I stood beside an RUC man, who was called Harry. I learned this, because one or two men out of every group knew him and shouted their greetings over to him.

Everybody was in good humour, the rain kept off, it was 'chancy-looking, showery-looking yet', Harry, said to me. Only the woman who painfully sang about 'The Blood of Jesus' as the parade went by seemed unhappy. The tent in the first field was full of beer drinkers and boys in kilts, who were delighted when a girl roared over at them: 'What's under your kilt?' Hamburgers were on sale, as well as instant colour photos, ice cream and cassette tapes of Orange songs. A big sign across the path of the parade read: 'Ballinamallard Says No', making clear the village's opposition to the Anglo-Irish Agreement.

The bands began to arrive at the field at midday, the assembly point, where they would be addressed by their leaders. The Orange Order, since the victory over the papist King James in 1690, had clearly developed skills in finding good fields for the assembly. This one, on the outskirts of Ballinamallard, made it seem as though God himself, smiling down on Orangemen, had moulded the field into a gentle slope, so that everyone could see. Orangemen, Orangewomen and their offspring sat down for a good rest. Big men unstrapped the drums from their waists. Children were having a field day, banging the drums without having to lift them. Banners were left resting on the ground. Kilts were carefully kept in place. Little packages which contained a sandwich, a bun and a paper napkin were on sale.

It was time for speeches. There was a special welcome for the Grand Masters who had come to Ballinamallard from the adjoining counties, the counties of the Orange diaspora: Cavan, Monaghan, Leitrim, Donegal, in the Republic of Ireland, which no longer had Twelfth of July parades. Then there was a moment of silence for an RUC man, a member of the Orange Order in Fermanagh, who had been killed recently by the IRA. He was the fourth member of his Lodge to be shot dead, and this year the Lodge had decided to stay away from the parade. Everybody stood in silence. 'God Our Strength in Ages Past' was sung.

Nobody listened much to the speeches which followed – they were too busy meeting old friends whom they hadn't seen since the previous year, sitting down beside them to talk. The speakers railed against the Anglo-Irish Agreement, one of them evoking the name of the people of Corinth to whom St Paul had addressed himself, who were besieged as the Protestants of Ulster were besieged. A small crowd stood around the stage and listened very attentively to all this. The final speaker was John Brooke, Lord Brookeborough, whose accent had not a single trace of Fermanagh in it.

In 1933 his father, a future Prime Minister of Northern Ireland, had addressed this same assembly in a different place on a previous Twelfth. The *Fermanagh Times* reported his speech. 'There was a great number of Protestants and Orangemen who employed Roman Catholics,' the paper reported him as saying. 'He felt he could speak freely on this subject as he had not a Roman Catholic about his own place . . . Roman Catholics were endeavouring to get in everywhere and were out with all their force and might to destroy the power and constitution of Ulster.

There was a definite plot to overpower the vote of Unionists in
the North. He would appeal to loyalists therefore, whenever possible, to employ good Protestant lads and lassies.' His son, fifty-
three years later, was rather more restrained and simply denounced
the Anglo-Irish Agreement in gentle tones.

The bands assembled again, full of good cheer. There was a
good night's drinking ahead for those who weren't members of
the temperance movement. The old tunes rang through the air,
including one whose opening notes bore a resemblance to a rebel
song from Wexford which I used to sing when I was a child. I
heard it all day; nearly every band had a go at playing it, and each
time I was sure that the devil himself, or the Pope perhaps, had
come among us and made the bands play the tune of 'The Boys
of Wexford'.

> We are the Boys of Wexford who fought with heart and hand
> To burst in twain the galling chain and free our native land.

But fortunately, after the opening few bars, the tune grew out of
all recognition into an Orange tune. No Pope here. I stood on
the bridge in Ballinamallard and watched the bands go by. The
banners showing the burning of the Protestant Martyrs Latimer
and Ridley with the words 'Suffer Death Rather Than Submit to
Popery' written up, and the slogan 'The Protestant Religion and
Open Bible We Will Maintain'.

I watched the bands from the South with great vigilance
until I spotted a band from Drum in County Monaghan and met
Nigel Johnston who worked at the Tyrone Guthrie Centre and
was part of the Drum entourage. I wanted a lift to Drum on the
Orange bus.

Nigel told me where the bus was, and I stood there waiting
for the Orange Band from Drum to arrive. I had been in Drum
on many occasions, always on a Saturday. There was always an
odd sense of quiet, slow decay in the village.

Being mainly Protestant, it had lost its natural hinterland in
Fermanagh. Bertie Anderson's pub in Drum had seen better days,
having been once a prosperous general village store. Now, it
opened only on a Saturday night, winter and summer, between
ten o'clock and twelve. The same few gentlemen came in every

week for a drink to discuss the affairs of the locality. Calendars from the early 1960s adorned the walls. One side of the bar had been a grocery, and all the drawers still had the names of what they used to hold embossed on them: tea, sugar, cloves, cinnamon. Now they were empty; things had changed.

The Drum band, when they arrived, was young, and there was a vitality about the way they played that would have done wonders for the atmosphere in Bertie Anderson's on a Saturday night. Their leader, who, through an appalling coincidence shared the name Gerry Adams with the President of Sinn Fein, agreed that they would give me a lift to Drum. He then directed the Orange band to form a circle and play 'The Sweet By and By' one more time. I stood and watched them. When they had finished they put their gear into the luggage compartment of the bus and came aboard.

Our bus then joined the queue of buses leaving Ballinamallard for points all over Fermanagh. Nigel told me that he was a member of Ian Paisley's Free Presbyterian Church, which had its only Southern Church in Drum.

At six o'clock the news came on the radio. A Catholic had been shot dead in Belfast by Protestant paramilitaries; the RUC, the bulletin said, were treating the murder as sectarian. The man was from Tyrone. There was silence on the bus, nobody looked up. After a while Nigel and myself resumed our conversation about hi-fis and stereo sound equipment, which we continued until we reached Lisnaskea, the last stop on the Northern side of the border.

The bus then crossed the border and drove into Clones, thereafter along the narrow roads to Drum. The Orange Hall was open. Friends and relations of the band stood around the street.

As they re-grouped, one band member asked his wife if she had milked the cows. When the band was ready they set off again, down the street of Drum, playing 'The Sweet By and By' once more, and then back up past us to the other end of the town playing 'The Sash My Father Wore'. There was a loneliness about them, and somehow a bravery for continuing to parade south of the border, so long after all the battles had been fought. They invited me into the Orange Hall for tea and sandwiches, which

I accepted, and when we had eaten our fill we moved across the
street to Bertie Anderson's pub which had opened as a special
mark of respect to the Twelfth of July, where we drank beer,
agreeing that it had been a wonderful Twelfth in Ballinamallard.

*

I was now back in County Monaghan, in Bernard Loughlin's
house, beside the Tyrone Guthrie Centre, a few miles from Drum.
Basil Lenaghan, who had joined us for dinner that thundering
evening in Ballinaleck, rang up one day and said he was going to
the Fleadh Ceoil — traditional music festival — in Ballyshannon
that weekend with his brother Noel. Did I want to go? A weekend
of music and drinking in Ballyshannon, at the very mouth of
Lough Erne, on the Atlantic Ocean, followed by a few days
walking? I said I'd love to go.

On Saturday I went to Ballyshannon, where I arrived in the
afternoon and booked into the local hotel. There was a great stir
in the town. This was the Ulster Fleadh, organized by Comhaltas
Ceolteoiri Eireann, the national organization which organizes and
fosters traditional Irish music. Last year the Ulster Fleadh had
been held on the northern side of the border at Warrenpoint, but
this year it was being held in the South, in another of the border
towns, Ballyshannon.

There was a time when traditional Irish music resembled the
Irish language: a worthy but dying cause, something worth con-
serving rather than using. The 1960s had changed all that. The
Fleadh Ceoil became a great hippy festival. A whole town would
be taken over for a long weekend, crowds would come from all
over the country. Some of them would have no interest in the
music whatsoever; they would be interested in the drinking,
which would go on all night under an extended licence, and the
possibility of fornication. 'Puritan Ireland's dead and gone',
wrote the poet John Montague of the 1963 Fleadh Ceoil in Mullingar.

Puritan Ireland had since reasserted itself somewhat, however,
to the benefit of traditional Irish music. A large number of young
people were now playing the old music with great seriousness
and skill. Drinking and fornication were still pursued, but more
quietly. Although most of the music had its origins in the nine-

teenth century and was also played by Protestants in the North, it was seen as part of the Gaelic heritage, the Catholic tradition.

Competitions in dimly lit halls would be run all weekend for every age group and every instrument, but the best part of the Fleadh would be the spontaneous sessions in pubs and hotels. Basil's brother Noel played the mandolin and the flute, as well as being a great singer, and he would be our passport for the weekend. Both Basil and Noel, big men with beards, were from Andersonstown. Basil had a big loud laugh, and when I ventured around Ballyshannon in search of the Lenaghans, I listened for Basil's laugh.

The town, right on the border not far from Belleek, was built on a steep hill. When I had eaten and had a short sleep, I walked up the hill, peering around the doors of various public houses, but there was no Basil and no Noel. Eventually, I found them in MacIntyre's. I put my head around the door and there they were: Noel, complete with flute, Basil, complete with loud laugh. Noel's French girlfriend Marie-Claire was also there. They moved over, found me space and I was sitting comfortably by the time the next tune started.

As the evening progressed, the players became used to each other; as soon as one of them started up a tune, the rest would follow. Most of the time the music was jaunty, but sometimes it was deeply melancholy. When the musicians grew tired they stopped and called on a woman who was standing at the door to sing. There wasn't a sound in the room while she sang; her voice was clear and true, the song a long story of the loved one gone into exile, leaving his love behind.

Eventually, Noel and Basil decided that we should move. We'd had our fill of drink and music in MacIntyre's. It was time to investigate what was going on in the town.

Every pub we passed had a session in full swing; musicians were playing on the streets. Every pub was full, and there were also sessions going on in every available space in the two hotels. A pub at the top of the town with a thatched roof seemed to be doing good business, and there seemed no point in trying to get a drink there. We went into a pub further out of the town on the opposite side of the street. We were greeted with silence.

This was the edge of the town which was taking no part in the Fleadh; the drinkers here took a dim view not only of the music, but also of the sort of people from all parts of the North who had invaded their town. Basil's loud laugh was viewed with deep suspicion too, and there was a prospect for a few moments that we would not be served. The pub was called McGinley's, and it seemed to pride itself on its regular customers and low-key, dull atmosphere.

Once the preliminaries were over, which involved us announcing where we were from, and where we were staying, Basil laughed some more, which caused even the most surly of the drinkers to take notice. What was the atmosphere down the town like? they wanted to know. We told them it was great, and they nodded their heads. A deep gloom pervaded the pub. Noel sang a song, which didn't lift the cloud much. A man sang 'The Moon Behind the Hill' in an old-fashioned tenor voice which seemed to spark off something in the pub. This was the sort of song which would have no place at the Fleadh down the town; Comhaltas Ceolteoiri Eireann wouldn't think much of it. It was old-fashioned, but it wasn't period enough or Irish enough to be traditional.

Another man followed it with 'Love Thee Dearest', a high Victorian ballad, and from then on the public house at the edge of the town started to have its own Fleadh, taking advantage of the extended licensing hours. Basil recited 'Shanahan's Oul' Shebeen' for them, and Noel played his flute. A woman tried to sing 'The Old Bog Road', but forgot the words. By the time we left, everyone had cheered up enormously.

The pubs were closing now. Basil, Noel and Marie-Claire were staying in the hotel across the road where the music was still going on. A full room listened in silence to a man who sang a song he had written on the morning of Bobby Sands's death on hunger strike. All eyes stared at the stranger; there was in the room the sort of heightened emotion and tension with which people still remember the hunger strikes of 1981.

Drink was still readily available, and drunks were wandering about the streets. Young people were hanging around my hotel with no idea where they were going to spend the night. The music was still going, the fiddlers, flute players and box players were still making music at three in the morning when I went to bed.

*

When I woke on Sunday morning, someone was playing an accordion beneath my window. It was a grey day which promised rain. The previous day I had avoided the competitions, but today I wanted to see two official parts of the Fleadh: the singing competitions for traditional songs and for newly composed ballads.

These were to take place at lunchtime in the local cinema. The singing was good. There was a superb version of 'The Flower of Sweet Strabane':

> O were I the king of Ireland and had all things at my will
> I'd roam through all creation your pleasure to find still
> And the pleasure I would seek the most I'd have you understand
> Is to win the heart of Martha, the flower of sweet Strabane

Each singer came to the top of the hall and stood beside the judges' table, singing several songs. The hall was half empty, and it was easy to sit back and wallow in these ballads, full of the names of places in the North, each one associated with love or the longings of exile. 'Bonny Lifford' was invoked, as well as 'some lonesome valley in the wildwoods of Tyrone'. Other songs told of the shores of 'Sweet Lough Erne', the 'Flower of Maherally' and the 'Craigie Hills'.

When the competition for new ballads began, a man stood up and sang a song with a refrain about 'my horses and plough'. When he had finished another man in the hall objected and said it wasn't the singer's own song, it had been written by someone else. He seemed sure about this and named the man whom he alleged had written the song. The singer sat down, somewhat cowed by the assertion that he was some sort of impostor. The matter was let rest because his song didn't feature among the winners; but it was a small, odd event in the day, this middle-aged man, alone in the hall, who had clearly come to Bally-shannon with a song written out in longhand, which he gave to the judges, then sang, falsely claiming it as his own. I watched

him as he walked out of the hall and didn't see him again that
day.

I spent the rest of the day wandering from pub to pub with
Noel, Basil and Marie-Claire. Once, when Noel started playing
in the back room of a pub, he was joined by a fiddler; the two
of them played for some time before they were joined by others
and a real session began. I took a walk out to the western side of
the town where the Erne flowed into the sea. The sun was going
down, but the day was still bright, most of the clouds had lifted.
Bundoran was just a few miles down the coast, the seaside resort
used by Northern Catholics. And out there was the Atlantic
Ocean, the next parish America.

*

The following morning I told the man in the newsagent's across
the bridge in Ballyshannon that I wanted to walk to Garrison,
in the North. He pointed to the main road and told me to go as
far as Belleek and then turn right. I told him that I wanted to go
along a side road which wasn't busy.

'The main road won't be busy either,' he said. The main road
led straight into the North and two Gardaí were stopping all cars.
I walked up the hill on the other side of the town and began to
make my way to Garrison by way of Lough Melvin.

It was a grey day, and there was mist on the mountains ahead.
Clearly, it was going to rain. I was on my own again now. Basil
had gone back to his wife and his child in Fermanagh, Noel and
Marie-Claire had returned to Belfast, but I was here in the midst
of fields full of thistles; the fields were divided by dry stone walls,
some of them had been cut for silage, others just left there, as
though their owners had abandoned them. All along the road
were newly built bungalows beside derelict houses.

Most of the bungalows had taken their design from a book
called *Bungalow Bliss*, which offered ready-made plans for seventy
variations on a basic bungalow plan, and thus removed the need
for an architect.

The author of *Bungalow Bliss*, Jack Fitzsimons, sat in the Senate
in Dublin. In his introduction to the book he wrote: 'For the
first four years of my life I lived in a two-roomed thatch cottage

rented by my father at two shillings per week. The floor area was about 300 square feet. The furniture consisted of a settle bed full of rubbish and rats, a table, iron bed and a few chairs. It had a front door and two tiny windows. Built in a hold on the side of a hill, if you can imagine such a situation, it blended into the landscape, surrounded by privet hedges, white thorn bushes and trees. I still have nostalgic memories of the cricket in the hearth and the high, thatched, smoke-blackened ceiling. But animals now would not be housed in such conditions.'

The Michelin map I was using did not include most of the small roads I came to, but I felt that if I kept going straight I would arrive at Lough Melvin. I knew I was getting close to the border because the road I was walking on began to deteriorate; the surface was in bad repair. I sat down for a while and listened to the one-thirty news on my small radio. Three RUC men had been killed by the IRA in Newry; James Molyneaux, the leader of the Official Unionist Party, had called on Britain to seal the border.

Suddenly, the lake came into view, I could see the calm water in the dull grey light. The land was mostly bog now, but the growth on the hedgerows was luscious. As I went on, the mountains on the opposite side came into view as well. The peaks were bare and rough. Thick clusters of trees were growing on an island on Lough Melvin. No cars passed and I met nobody on the road. Dark clouds still hung overhead. The road grew narrow until it became a lane. A stream flowing into the lake was the colour of strong tea, and as I came closer to the lake itself, its colour changed from the reflected grey of the sky to the dark bog brown of its own water.

At the border, I saw that a huge immoveable chunk of concrete with rusty iron bars coming out of it had been placed on a bridge; to blow up the concrete would mean taking out the bridge as well. The few yards of road between this slab of concrete and the next had disintegrated completely and turned to muck; I tried hard not to slip on it as I walked into the North. The road was overhung with trees, and there was a definite sense that no one had been here for a long time. I passed an abandoned cottage.

I walked up the avenue towards the first house I saw on the

left-hand side of the road. I was afraid at first, but was much encouraged by a tricolour in an upstairs window. As I approached, several dogs ran towards me and surrounded me, preventing me getting any further. I glanced at all the windows of the house, expecting to see a face, but no one appeared. I edged forward, the dogs following me, still barking, clearly intent on stopping me getting too near. Eventually, a young fellow with an English accent came to the window. He came out into the yard and called off the dogs.

The house was being decorated, he apologized as he invited me inside for a cup of tea. An older man was in the kitchen as well. I explained to them my mission, and they seemed to think it sounded plausible. They explained that most of the area was nationalist, with certain exceptions. Some of the exceptions had had their houses blown up since the Troubles started, they said. There had also been a long battle fought over the border crossing, they explained. At one stage local people had brought in contractors from all parts of the country in the middle of the night to re-open the road and, for a time, people were driving freely through. Then, after the killing of an RUC man in Enniskillen, the army came again and added the concrete to the bridge, which had made the road-block effective and difficult to clear.

Garrison, they said, used to be a busy village in the tourist season: the fishing on Lough Melvin was excellent, but the hotels had been blown up by the IRA and it was a ghost town now. There had been thirty-one houses in this townland twenty years before, the older man told me, and now there were only seven. People were getting out.

Was there anything else I wanted to know? they asked. No, I said I was okay. They both agreed that there was a woman I should visit on my way into Garrison, she was a great character. Although both her father and her husband had been in the British army, no harm had ever been done to her, nor ever would be. She did her shopping in all the Catholic shops in Garrison and she employed Catholics in her house. People respected her for that. They gave me precise directions to her house, which was on an island on the lake, with a small causeway which made it accessible from the shore. The house was worth looking at as well, they said. She probably wouldn't mind me calling.

I followed their directions, and I turned down a long, tree-lined drive. The vegetation was thick on either side, and only at intervals could I see that I was walking along a causeway. A small boat was moored at the edge of the lake and there seemed to be a thick forest behind the house.

The house itself was modest, with a wooden exterior, cleanly painted, with big windows. I passed by a room painted bright pink, with a small bed and a painting of ships on the wall. There was a porch at the other side and the front door was wide open. I rang a bell, but there was no one in. The gardens were well kept, and when I had walked a few yards towards the forest, I met the gardener. The lady of the house was away for the day, he said, she would be back tomorrow. I looked at him, realizing that he must be one of the Catholic employees I had been told about. I asked him if it was far to Garrison and he said it was just a few miles. The rain had started now, but after a mile or so it lifted. The sky was still dark, however, and it was obvious that the rain would come back.

The road began to improve. A small cottage was surrounded by broken-up cars, which were also strewn along the roadside. The owner of the cottage who made his living from spare parts told me that he never went into Garrison any more for a drink. Even though it was more expensive in Ballyshannon, he'd prefer to go in there. You'd have more peace, he said. Garrison was finished, he said; two of the roads into the town were now blocked – it used to be a thriving little village. A few children came out to look at me. They were the youngest, he said; he had ten altogether.

As I came nearer to Garrison, I passed a machine for trimming the hedges and keeping them in order. There was a smell of cut grass now and there were swarms of midges flying around my head. A man in a tractor passed me, but otherwise there was no traffic.

Garrison was fast asleep. I went into the first pub I saw, which was deserted. The man behind the bar stood back and sized me up for a minute before he asked me what I wanted. I told him I wanted a pint of beer. He pulled the pint slowly, looking up at me suspiciously. I told him that I had walked from Ballyshannon, and was now looking for a place to stay. I asked him if he knew of anywhere. Yes, he did, he said, there was a place just across the bridge, a brand new place, built by Fermanagh District Council – a sort of hostel for hikers.

When I finished my drink I wandered across. Inside the door there was a café with a lanky blond man in his twenties and a dark woman, whom I thought was Egyptian, holding a child seated at a table.

The hostel had just opened. I was told that I could have my dinner there, and that if I had any wet clothes there was a drying room specially for them. The whole place was covered in a brand new grey carpet. Upstairs in a big, high dormitory there were duvets on all the beds, and red sheets. The blond man introduced himself as Edwin, and told me that there was hot water at all times; he gave me a key in case I would be out late. His wife, who was in fact Iranian, was going to make a vegetarian goulash for dinner. I could eat with them, if I wished. There was, he said, only one other person staying in the hostel.

This was the last thing I expected to find in Garrison. A purpose-built hostel, with facilities for caravans and camping, with a grey and red motif running right through the building, with smaller dormitories for families as well as large men's and women's dormitories. He and his wife, Edwin said, were members of the Bahai religion, so the business of being a Catholic or a Protestant didn't really matter. I asked him how many times people had asked whether he was a Protestant Bahai or a Catholic Bahai. People said this all the time, he told me, everybody thought it was a great joke. He said that he had been in school in Portora, so I knew he was a Protestant Bahai.

I went to see a local who was a Catholic farmer. His children went by bus into the Catholic school in Enniskillen. He remembered Garrison as a busy village in the fishing season. There were two hotels; one had been blown up by the IRA, the other had burnt down; there had also been a hostel which was blown up by the IRA. The fishermen who came every year were mostly English and once the Troubles started, they never came back so there was no point in rebuilding the hotels. He was curious about the hostel; he had heard that it was being run by 'a wee Prod'. I told him that Edwin was a member of the Bahai religion. 'For the people who live around here, he's a wee Prod,' he said. Some in the locality, he added, would be offended that a job like that had been given to a Protestant.

I remarked that I hadn't seen the British army or the police on the road. They didn't come in by land any more, he told me; the area was too dangerous. They flew in by helicopter. There were strict divisions between Catholics and Protestants in this area, he said. If Catholic land went up for sale, no Protestant would be let bid for it and vice versa. All the same, farms were getting bigger; as people emigrated, neighbours bought the land.

The kids were sitting in the living room listening to all this, as well as trying to watch a programme on the big colour television. We had tea and cake.

My host was brought up here. When he was young, he thought times were always going to be hard. He had no inkling then of the relative prosperity he lived in now, the comfort of a well-heated bungalow, the bigger farm, the grants, the children brought to secondary school by bus. He sat back and shook his head in wonder at how things had changed.

The local priest, he told me, didn't like the name Garrison. It sounded too English. So he tried to have it changed to Devinish, but he couldn't. Instead, he changed the name of the local football team to Devinish.

The following morning I rang Mrs Gregory, the woman who lived in the house on the small island I had called at the day before. Mrs Gregory invited me out for lunch, so I retraced my steps in the direction of Ballyshannon until I came to the gate which led down to the causeway.

Mrs Gregory was full of information about Garrison. She had come here first with her father fifty years before for the fishing. The fishing was wonderful between the wars. Everyone knew everybody else, came to the same hotel at the same time of year and in the evening as they were having drinks before dinner in the bar of Casey's Hotel or McGovern's Hotel all the fish caught that day would be laid out on the table. Things were different then. If you caught a particularly good fish, you could have it wrapped and posted to England, and the post office was so efficient that it would arrive at its destination still edible. You couldn't do that now.

The gillies were cheap then as well. They were all local and they knew Lough Melvin inside out; if you got a good gillie, he would take you to the best places. Now the gillies cost a small fortune. Mrs Gregory's son came in and joined us for lunch. We had beer and cold meat and salad with a good dressing. I was delighted with this account of Garrison in the 1930s, straight out of a novel by Somerset Maugham or J. G. Farrell. Yes, things had changed, Mrs Gregory said. Why, there was a fishing competition recently in Lough Melvin, for which droves of fishermen arrived on a bus from Belfast. She had heard on good authority that the winning fish was not quite defrosted. Nothing like that would ever have happened in the old days.

She tried to do what shopping she could now in the local shops, she said. By 'local' I knew she meant Catholic. What she couldn't get in the local shops, she bought in Belleek.

She showed me around the house. Every room was in perfect condition. There were flowers everywhere. She rented half the house to fishermen at various times of the year and did bed and breakfast. She gave me her brochure in case I ever wanted to come back. I thanked her for the lunch, after which her son drove me as far as Garrison.

The sky was a brooding grey, promising rain again, hanging low over the lake as I walked out of Garrison towards Rossinver in the South. Almost immediately the road began to deteriorate into a damp, narrow lane, full of pools and puddles, muck and mire. Soon I came to the old familiar sight, the huge, heavy slab of rough concrete with iron fenders rising towards the sky. Garrison was closed off from its hinterland on two sides – no wonder the pub had been so empty.

The road had become run-down with lack of use, and it was some time before the mucky surface gave way to something more solid. The fields around here looked in bad shape, with clumps of rushes growing all over the grass and a sense of the bog everywhere. The mountains on the opposite side of the lake were a dark green, and the lake was now choppy; the wind was starting up. There were two cars parked outside a bungalow, which had a clear view over the lake from all the front windows. A man came out to collect a pair of waders from the boot of one of the cars. He had the look of a city man in the country, a man on his fishing holiday.

I could hear the noise of children roaring in the distance: it sounded like a football match. I went down a lane towards the lake, where there was a small beach, a mixture of gravel and sand, and about thirty pale, white-skinned children wading in the water. Only two or three were swimming. The rest of them were standing there, shivering under the brutal grey of the sky. I looked along the shore, and instantly understood what was going on. Swimming lessons. The two men who stood watching the bathers had all the look of teachers, or youth workers. Those who were swimming had an instructor beside them, miming the gestures required. The rest just stood in the freezing water, waiting. Their bodies were completely white; in fact, there was a lack of colour in the whole scene, the grey sky, grey lake, grey gravel and the pale backs of the kids who were up to their waists in the water. I passed by the old ruin of a church at the end of the beach as I walked back towards the road.

Rossinver consisted of a pub, a shop, a post office, a petrol pump and a few houses. I bought a bar of chocolate in the shop and turned left out of the village. I was now in County Leitrim on the road to Kiltyclogher, climbing up a steep hill. There were no cars on the road, except a Garda car and two Irish army lorries which passed me going in the opposite direction. The previous week, the Taoiseach Garret FitzGerald had come to Leitrim to encourage the locals to grow trees. Trees had become a deeply emotional issue in Leitrim, as private investors became involved in buying up land for forestry.

Farmers whose families had tilled a thirty-acre plot for generations were dismayed to find that their neighbours had sold up, and the farm beside them was to become a forest. The land was bad – probably the worst in the country. The soil, however, was the best in Europe for the growing of spruce trees. Efficiency and modernity demanded that the land be used for the growing

of trees. History and basic human feeling demanded that the
families should be kept on the land, that each piece of land was
a piece of heritage, to be used by the small farmers.

I walked along through the boggy terrain where a few
scrawny-looking haystacks lay in the fields, through the landscape
dotted with abandoned houses, and stretches of new forests. There
was no sense of habitation anywhere, the population of Leitrim
having decreased from 150,000 to 27,000 between 1841 and 1986
because of emigration, famine, and now forestry. I understood
why the forests had become an emotional issue. I thought of de
Valera's famous St Patrick's Day broadcast in 1943, when he
wished for 'a land whose countryside would be bright with cosy
homesteads, whose fields and villages would be joyous with the
sounds of industry, with the rompings of sturdy children, the con-
tests of athletic youths and the laughter of comely maidens, whose
firesides would be forums for the wisdom of serene old age. It
would, in a word, be the home of a people living the life that
God desires that man should live.'

Forty years later the road between Rossinver and Kiltyclogher,
the heart of rural Ireland, was a convincing testament to the
failure of de Valera's vision, which seemed now like a joke from
a bitter satirical sketch. He wasn't a drinking man, but it is likely
that even he would have taken a dim view of the plight of
the publicans of Kiltyclogher, right on the border with County
Fermanagh. There were six pubs in the town, and four were
closed completely for lack of trade, one was open only at the
weekends and the other, where I drank to de Valera's poor old
ghost, was the only hostelry in the town which was open all day.
And even here trade was bad on weekdays, the owner told me.

One of the signatories of the 1916 Proclamation, Sean Mac
Diarmada, who was later executed, was born near Kiltyclogher,
and there was a monument commemorating him at the crossroads
in the village. His house up the mountain was also a monument,
the man behind the bar told me; it had been preserved for
posterity, but the man who held the key to it wasn't there any
more. He agreed that preserving the cottage of the patriot while
the abandoned houses of the natives fell down all around was an
odd thing to do. People were leaving all the time, he said, not

just young people, but entire families. People wouldn't even bother putting their houses up for sale; they just left them, and the houses gradually fell down.

There was no trade from the North any more, he said. The bridge which connected the North and the South at the bottom of the town had been blown up, and there was just a footbridge now. Over the years there had been a few bombs in Kiltyclogher. The local dance hall had been blown up. He said he didn't know who was responsible. The lack of a direct route into the North didn't just affect the trade in the town, he told me; it made a huge difference to farmers who had land on both sides. They now had to drive twenty miles to get to land which was just a stone's throw across the river.

It was easier to live in the North. 'They're getting paid for living over there,' he said, referring to the grants available on the other side of the border.

The sky was clearing now in the late afternoon. There had been no rain. I passed the monument to Sean Mac Diarmada and walked down towards the river. I realized that I had taken a wrong turn – there was no footbridge here. When I looked at the river, it struck me that it would be easy to cross here, with animals or a jeep. There was a car parked at the footbridge, the owner had clearly left it here and walked to the other side. The bridge had been destroyed.

There was a long lonely lane between the river and the main road. Although it was well after six, the sun came out and it became quite warm and still. There was a man coming towards me on the road. I felt uneasy about him. The loneliness of the place gave me the creeps. I was tired now, and I regretted not having stayed in Kiltyclogher for the night. He was walking towards me in a way which was deliberate and ominous. I considered turning back. I stared straight at him as he came close. 'It rains oftentimes,' he said, as he passed me by. He looked like a swain from a Thomas Hardy poem. I walked on towards the main road, ashamed at having been so fearful.

The road here was well paved, and the fields seemed to be bigger; the soil of better quality than in the South, although there were forests here as well at intervals along the road. In a field beside a new bungalow, a man was spreading some sort of weed-killer. I talked to him for a while about the weather and the better grants in the North. He told me that there was a guest house between here and Belcoo, which was a good five miles away, he said. I asked him if he had any land in the South and he said he did. How did he get to it? Did he have to drive around by Belcoo and Blacklion, as the man in the pub had said? No, he said, there was a narrow stretch of water beyond the old bridge at Kiltyclogher and it was possible to get a car across there as well as animals. I described to him the stretch of water I had come across when I took a wrong turn. He told me, yes, that was the place.

A calm had come down over the countryside, lit by the late evening sun. My feet were sore now, and my back hurt, and I was miles away thinking of something else when I caught the first glimpse of Lough Macnean. It glittered in the sun. The sky was now almost completely blue, with a few white clouds on the horizon. There was a shine over everything, which was strange after the greyness of the days, the brooding sky I had been walking under.

I suddenly felt an enormous sense of relief. I couldn't stop looking around me at the way the light lay on the land, the way the warmth of the sky sharpened the blue of the lake. I wandered along towards Belcoo, ignoring the directions I had been given for the guest house. I didn't want to stop. I was riveted by the pleasure of this: the tiredness, the calmness of the evening, the new lake, the brightness. I could feel my senses becoming sharper, my eyes noticing the shifts of light.

6

Enniskillen and South Fermanagh

It was a dirty day, bleak, full of drizzle and mist. I had my breakfast in the guest house in Blacklion, went to the door and looked over the lake outside, but I could find nothing of the previous evening's pleasure. It was depressing. Winston Churchill was wrong when he went on about the 'dreary steeples of Fermanagh'; the steeples were a riot of colour and excitement compared with the dreariness of the lakes. I stood at the door of the guest house staring at the integrity of the quarrel between Upper and Lower Lake Macnean, which met at the bridge between Blacklion and Belcoo. A grim day. I didn't feel like walking anywhere.

I went back into the house and asked the owner's daughter what time the bus went to Enniskillen. You don't use buses here, she said. What do you use? I asked. You go over to the Gardaí who are guarding the border, she said, they stop every car which is going into the North, and you ask them to find you a car which will take you as a passenger. Do they not mind? I asked her. She insisted that this was the normal method of transport for those who didn't have a car of their own. I wanted her to go out and ask for me, but she refused. I stood for a while watching a young Garda and his middle-aged colleague stop the cars. It was difficult to tell whether what the girl said was true or not. I could be arrested for distracting a Garda from the course of his duty.

After a while I wandered casually over to the two men in blue. The younger one was interrogating the driver of a lorry, and looked around at me as I asked the older man if he knew of a lift to Enniskillen. Just as the older Garda was looking puzzled, the younger one turned again and said: 'This man'll take you.' The lorry driver nodded in agreement. The girl in the guest house was right, and I gave three silent cheers to the police force of the Republic of Ireland as I walked around to the passenger side of the lorry.

He dropped me right in the middle of Enniskillen. There was still a light drizzle falling. I went into William Blake's and had a drink to cheer myself up. I bought a newspaper and wandered around as a man of leisure. My feet were slightly sore, but otherwise there was nothing wrong with me. I went up past Blake's until I came to a narrow lane going up a steep hill.

At the top there was a building which had clearly belonged to the army at a certain stage. I passed a yellow station-wagon, parked at the side. The car belonged to the painter Felim Egan, whose studio was here in this building. I went in and up the stairs. I knocked on the door of the first landing. I could hear footsteps across the bare floorboards. I had disturbed him; I knew he would be working now. He opened the door, the look of someone preoccupied on his face. He was painting.

The windows were covered with thick sheets of plastic; the strip lighting in the big high room had all the power of daylight, but was more consistent. There were new paintings all around the walls. The paintings were cool, considered, careful, tactful. Smooth colours were applied thinly on canvas and the smoothness was broken by lines, grids, arcs which were themselves broken and made to reappear.

He was working, as well, on a set of watercolours. The basic grey in them was the same blue-grey as the sky in Fermanagh, but there was a gap in each one as a line like a river, or a fork of lightning, ripped down through the grey watercolour. All summer as I came and went, the paintings on the wall changed, some were taken down and brought to an exhibition in West Cork; others were altered radically; others were left there, with new lines added, subtle changes made. Felim kept doing new watercolours. He worked, too, on a collaboration with the poet Seamus Heaney. Heaney had given him words to work from: Tree, No Tree, Chestnut Tree, Soul Tree, Thorn Tree, Wishing Tree. He had told him about a set of poems he was working on where the loss of parents was seen as empty spaces where certain trees had stood. He told him about a tree in Ardboe, near Lough Neagh, a wishing tree, to which people came and nailed coins or religious medals, and as the bark grew the tree began to reject the metal.

We drove out to the Killyhevlin Hotel to have lunch. The Erne outside was a deep brown, full of mud. I hadn't seen it like that before. 'I do not know much about gods,' I said to Felim when we came outside after lunch, 'but I think that the river is a strong brown god.' I told him that the line was from T. S. Eliot's *Four Quartets*. That afternoon while I was swimming in the L-shaped swimming pool in Enniskillen, he did a new water-colour with a brown undertone to the usual grey. He called it 'Brown God'.

He lived in a three-storey Victorian house looking on to the river with the painter Janet Pierce and her three children. During my sojourns in Enniskillen I slept in Janet's studio at the back of the house.

Rory, Janet's son, attended Portora up the road, and was full of information about what was to be seen locally. Janet's two daughters seemed to observe my coming and going with curiosity and wonder.

*

The new theatre at Enniskillen, the Ardhowen, was a great novelty. It had been opened the previous spring, an opening attended by the cream of local society. A man from Sinn Fein, Paul Corrigan, made one of the opening speeches; some of it was in Irish. Corrigan had become Chairman of the Fermanagh District Council, to the consternation of the local Protestants. 'It was a dark day,' one of them said to me.

The Catholic majority in Fermanagh had long been a thorn in the side of the Unionists, to put it mildly. At a meeting in Enniskillen in April 1948, the Unionist MP, E. C. Ferguson, for example, had this to say: 'The Nationalist majority in the County Fermanagh . . . stands at 3,604. I would ask the meeting to auth-orize their executive to adopt whatever plans and take whatever steps, however drastic, to wipe out this Nationalist majority.'

The hunger strike of 1981 had brought Sinn Fein into politics; Bobby Sands had won a seat in this constituency; after his death his election agent, Owen Carron, had also won the seat; Sinn

Fein was now busy consolidating its position. Sinn Fein and the
SDLP now ran local government in Fermanagh. A bust of Wolfe
Tone, the leader of the United Irishmen in the 1798 Rebellion,
was put up in the council chamber. The Sinn Fein members, all six
of them, had pledged support for the IRA campaign of violence. It
was a strange position for the RUC and UDR, some of whose
colleagues had been the victims of the IRA, and for the Unionists
who worked for the council to have to meet with and take
instructions from Sinn Fein.

One advantage of Sinn Fein's position of power in Fermanagh
was the safety of council buildings from IRA bombs. Ten years
previously, a hostel in Garrison would have been blown up by
the IRA, now it was effectively and legitimately controlled
by them. Likewise the new theatre in Enniskillen, designed by an
architect from Derry, was in no danger from bombs.

The theatre looked on to the Erne at the point where the old
railway bridge used to be. There was a season of films on in the
theatre which included Visconti's *The Damned*, which I had seen
before, remembering the slow corruption of everything in the
film, as history takes over in Germany, carrying the weak as well
as the strong in its current. I went to see it with Janet and Felim.

We thought we were late, and I had been telling them about
the beginning of the film, the orange glow of the melting steel
of the factory which would make arms for Hitler as the opening
sequence, but I needn't have done so, because the film started
late. There was a good reason for this: there were only two other
people in the theatre, which seated three hundred. The lure of
Visconti had left Fermanagh untouched. Even Blake's pub, to
which we retired after the movie, was quiet.

History had made Fermanagh quiet; again and again I experi-
enced the quietness of the streets of Enniskillen outside business
hours. Nobody was on the streets. It was like a town in the
early hours of the morning, before the milkman started on his
round. The British army were never seen in Enniskillen, the town
was policed entirely by the RUC. They walked with rifles up and
down on the street outside Janet and Felim's house.

*

One wet morning Felim and I drove down the main road to Florencecourt in search of the Marble Arch caves. They had been made accessible to the public, courtesy of Fermanagh District Coucil, who were taking advantage of the lavish EEC grants for general improvements in tourist amenities.

The car park was full; we joined the queue inside for the next guided tour. A map of the terrain below ground came free with the ticket. We were led down to where the rock was slimy, almost tender, to where the air was cold and damp. We sat in a boat and were brought sailing along underground by a guide, who told jokes. The caves were well lit, and it seemed unimaginable that cave divers had come here for sport when there were no lights. I tried to stop thinking about it, and concentrated on the pleasanter aspects of the caves, how rock formations came to resemble various objects, how much the whole thing looked like a collection of weird molten genitalia.

The underground river rose high in the winter, so that the caves could only be open in the summer. The guide took us along a Moses walk, a corridor cut low through the pool where the water was at a level with the top of the walls on either side. The rock above could be seen perfectly reflected in the calm, dead water. There wasn't a single movement in the water. Fish made their way in sometimes, but the darkness affected them; they didn't need their colour, the guide said. The skin of the brown trout, for example, lost its pigment here, and the fish became white, a lost soul wandering around in the dark, knowing no rest, no companionship, no ease; its small, puzzled consciousness nosing around in the still waters of the Marble Arch caves.

I didn't like being down there very much; the terror of being trapped never left me, and I was relieved when we climbed back up into daylight. It was still drizzling in the world outside. Felim wanted to drive to Boa Island on Lough Erne to see the Boa Island figure, which I had missed during the trip on Lough Erne.

He had been to Boa Island before, so he knew where to look for the figure. I would never have found it alone. The island was connected to the mainland by a bridge; a small wooden sign pointed to Caldragh Cemetery. It was raining now. The figure, sculpted in light red sandstone, sat among the undergrowth, with a vivid, slightly fierce look on its face. It was pre-Christian. It was here before all the monks. It was here before all the saints, scholars, high crosses and ruined churches. Its squat form sat on an ugly stone plinth among the long grass and the graves and the blackthorn bushes.

There was also a face on the other side; it was a Janus head, a double-edged sword. The side which faced back towards Enniskillen, however, was half spoiled, its glare was rather more intense and hurt. It looked as though if you were here late at night, it might eat you, or work wonders for you.

We stared at these live remnants of the Celtic past. There was a smaller figure standing beside the Janus head; someone had pencilled in the eyes and mouth – it was clear that the person responsible would have no luck. Felim was working hard on the collaboration with Seamus Heaney. He made the poet write out a poem in longhand; he thought of erasing it, crossing it out and drawing over it. He drove out in search of certain trees, and drew them in pencil. He went to Dublin and talked to Seamus Heaney, coming back with the new poems which Heaney had written about trees, and an introduction for the catalogue:

> I thought of walking round and round a space
> Utterly empty, utterly a source
> Where the decked chestnut tree had lost its place
> In our front hedge above the wallflowers.

The catalogue to mark the first stage of the collaboration was at the printers; the paintings, including the new watercolours, were to be hung in the Ardhowen Theatre, where Seamus Heaney would read the new poems.

I was still hanging around Enniskillen that evening, and I wandered into Blake's pub for a drink. The writer John McGahern sat at the bar. There had been a possibility that Seamus Heaney wouldn't be able to turn up, and John had agreed to deputize. I told him that Heaney had arrived, as I had just seen him in Janet and Felim's house. He seemed relieved, and had a drink.

McGahern lived on the other side of the border in a small, remote house overlooking a lake. Enniskillen was a sort of capital for him. He knew Blake's well. It had been his address during the marathon postal strike in the Republic in the late 1970s. He still had a quantity of Blake's own twenty-five-year-old whiskey which he had purchased over the years; Blake's had none left. I sampled it once at McGahern's house; it was like silk. He had written so well, so accurately, in such detail, about the world just south of the border that his work was almost more real than the places themselves. It was a time when the police had nothing to do except arrest cyclists for having no lights, when there were no cars on the road, when personal isolation and pain found no comfort in the monolith which southern Ireland had become.

Earlier in the year, in a lecture, he had spoken of Ireland in the early days of independence: 'The true history of the thirties, forties and fifties in this country has yet to be written. When it does, I believe it will be shown to have been a very dark time indeed, in which an insular church colluded with an insecure State to bring about a society that was often bigoted, intolerant, cowardly, philistine and spiritually crippled.'

We went out to the reading in the Ardhowen, where Seamus Heaney stood at the podium in the new theatre. I had seen him read many times before, and witnessed his soft way of pulling the audience with him, the mellifluous Derry accent, the slow grin. Tonight, he seemed uneasy, working harder with the audience, trying to explain himself. Even the poems he chose seemed more difficult and complex than the poems he usually read.

He talked about Felim Egan's painting of Hercules and Antaeus, as a metaphor for what was happening in the North. Hercules as force, outside strength, but Antaeus having to touch the earth before strength came, taking nourishment from the surrounding territory. He read his poem 'Hercules and Antaeus':

> Hercules lifts his arms
> in a remorseless V,
> his triumph unassailed
> by the powers he has shaken
> and lifts and banks Antaeus
> high as a profiled ridge,
> a sleeping giant,
> pap for the dispossessed

When the reading was over, Heaney was approached by dozens of people who wanted him to sign copies of his books. He talked to anyone who came near; he was genial, affable, at ease after the reading.

Afterwards there was a big dinner for all concerned in Franco's Italian restaurant. I watched John McGahern getting into his car to go home. Big dinners weren't his sort of thing. He had become, over the years, a connoisseur of quietness. He would go to Paris for a week or two in November, and to Canada for a while in the new year, but mostly he would stay on his small farm in Leitrim, with a weekly journey to Enniskillen.

*

Enniskillen throughout the summer was a good vantage point from which to view the fortunes of the Tyrone football team. On my first Sunday there in July I went to a match in Irvingstown, eight miles west of Enniskillen, to see a game of Gaelic football between Cavan and Tyrone.

As far as the Gaelic Athletic Association was concerned, Tyrone and Cavan were both in Ulster – the original Ulster which had nine counties – and the winner of this match would go on to play in the Ulster final. Gaelic football and hurling matches in the North had attractions beyond the excitement of the game; the matches were expressions of the Irish identity of the players and spectators. Members of the security forces in the North were banned by the GAA from joining the Association or playing its games: this was for Catholics only.

The programme gave the name of the counties in Irish, and the spectators stood for the Irish National Anthem, *The Soldier's Song*, before the game began. The BBC, however, despite the Irish identity of players, was here to record the game, and there was an official announcement that for those who wanted to see it again, the game would be replayed at six-fifteen that evening on BBC Northern Ireland. It is highly improbable, however, that anyone would want to see it, as the game was dull and the excitement minimal. When Tyrone went ahead, the crowd began to drift away during the second half; even a late goal didn't seem to interest many people. The general feeling was that Tyrone, despite its victory over Cavan, would get nowhere.

The general feeling was wrong. Tyrone were to go on to win the Ulster Final, later defeating the Connaught champions, Galway, to make their way to the All-Ireland Final. Hopes were high, even though the Kerry team whom they met in the final were considered almost invincible. In interviews before the big day later in the summer, many of the Tyrone players dedicated their game to the Republican prisoners in Long Kesh. They nearly beat Kerry; for the entire first half they ran away with the game. It would have been a great victory for Ulster and a great day for nationalists in the North, but the Kerry players' killer instinct, amazing coordination and almost magical power to be in the right place when the ball came, finally won the day.

★

Towards the end of July, I abandoned the fleshpots of Enniskillen and took a bus to Blacklion, saluting the two cops – whose colleagues earlier that month had so kindly procured a lift for me – and turned left along what was deemed a concession road. That meant there was no customs post or army post, but it was the North now and not the South, although no immediate difference was apparent.

It had been raining for several days; the black clouds had finally broken. 'The only thing for it is the high stool,' a man said to me. I agreed with him and passed on. There was a good ten miles between Blacklion and the next high stool – the next public house; it was already mid-afternoon. The fields were bigger and in better shape than any I had seen since Strabane. Fat cattle lolled about, and the rich pasture land was interspersed with bits of bogland.

I passed by several streams, noticing that the water was becoming clearer now as I moved east, with a light brown tinge in the water, rather than the previous strong tea. On the other side of the lake there was a bungalow built into the hill, surrounded by trees which must have had a clear view for miles of Upper and Lower Lough Macnean. I passed by an entry to the Ulster Way, a trail for serious walkers who enjoyed the great outdoors, the uphill struggle, the raw countryside, forests dripping with rain, soggy paths and adventures with wild animals. I was glad that I enjoyed none of these things, and thus kept to the road, hoping to make the town of Swanlinbar before night.

The land leading down to the lake on the left side of the road was still well kept and rich; the land on the other side led up to the hills and seemed soggy, as though the rain would lie on it for weeks before seeping slightly underground where it would wait patiently for a long time.

Closer to Florencecourt, I met a man who was doing up an old schoolhouse. He had bought it for half nothing, and was doing the work himself. There was another old schoolhouse further along, he said. The rain had eased and we stood there talking. After a while I felt brave enough to ask who owned the land around here. Most of the land, he said, was owned by Protestants. All the land on the left side of the road was in Protestant hands. On the other side, on the higher ground, the farms were Catholic, he said.

He knew a man, he told me, who smuggled a television along this road every weekend and brought it into the South. It was easy – there were hardly ever any checkpoints on the road; but one weekend he was caught, and they impounded the car and, of course, the television.

The nearest pub, he said, was in Blacklion in the South, and although the prices were higher, he often went there. The South was okay, he said. I gathered from the way he was talking that he was a Protestant. But recently he had been in a pub when a local man had come in selling *An Phoblacht*, the Sinn Fein newspaper which gloried in the deeds of the IRA, and asked him to buy one. He had felt a bit uneasy as he refused.

Evening was coming in early. He said that the nearest place ahead where a bed could be found was Swanlinbar, still a good seven miles away. It would be dark in an hour, by which time I would have reached the main Enniskillen–Swanlinbar road.

I was afraid of walking in the dark for two reasons. Firstly, I didn't want to meet a UDR patrol. Secondly, there had been a number of serious accidents in the area which involved pedestrians walking at night; one in which three youngsters were killed had happened nearby just a few days before. People drove on the side roads as though they were main roads, and they drove on the main roads like there was no tomorrow. Walking at night was looking for trouble.

I noticed a sign on the pole which said 'Forward to Victory: Join the Ulster Clubs'. As I moved along the sign appeared again and again. The Ulster Clubs, set up just before the signing of the Anglo-Irish Agreement, were a Protestant body who bitterly opposed the Agreement. Later in the year, a Protestant organiz- ation, close to the Ulster Clubs, would issue a statement saying that anyone from the Republic was a legitimate target in the North. Now, that threat was unstated but present, lurking under the rhetoric of various Protestant leaders.

When I came across the word 'Paisley' written in white letters across the road I knew that I had better stop wandering about in the dark. The word Paisley meant many things. I understood that here across this road in an area where most of the land was held by Protestants, during the summer months, the marching season, in the first year of the Anglo-Irish Agreement, there was a small edge of menace to the word. It was getting dark now, and I was still a good distance from the main road; I didn't know how far. There were no cars on the road.

I was surprised to see a sign for Bed and Breakfast just ahead. I had been assured by several people that there was no place to stay on this road. There was a long lane running down to a substantial new two-storey house, which looked well kept, warm and comfortable. Needless to say, I turned down towards this oasis and removed my cap as I rang the doorbell, hoping not to be mistaken for a tramp by the owners.

Even as the door opened I could feel the warm air. The woman was young and had the look of someone whose health had been much improved by country living. Ruddy cheeks and a well-fed, plump body. She seemed happy enough that I wanted a room for the night, and inquired if I wanted a meal as well. I wanted everything that was going. She said that there was soup, chicken and vegetables, sweet, followed by tea and coffee. I told her it sounded wonderful as she showed me to my room, and pointed the way to the bathroom should I need to avail myself of that facility. I took off my shoes and lay down on the bed. I could easily have fallen straight asleep, too tired even to eat; the heavy air of Fermanagh was having its effect. I forced myself to get up and see what was going on downstairs.

The house was decorated in the style now customary all over Ireland: multi-coloured carpets, multi-coloured curtains, multi-coloured wallpaper, multi-coloured pictures on the wall. No one, surrounded by so much colour, could remember their ancestors, or their immediate forebears, without considerable pride and joy at how much things had improved. No more mud cabins, no more Puritan grey; Protestant and Catholic united in layer after layer of colours, carpets patterned in squares of red and yellow, wallpaper in long stripes of blue and gold, curtains in vivid pink and white. Riots of colour.

A man from Omagh, on tour with his wife, was discussing sheep with the landlady's husband, a genial-looking fellow, who was a farmer. I sat at an adjoining table enjoying the soup. Another man came in, whose wife wasn't well and was lying down upstairs. They were on tour as well, and had been to see the caves, as had the couple from Omagh. I discovered that this house had only just opened as a bed and breakfast and was doing well because of its proximity to the caves. When they discovered I was from the South, they seemed pleased that someone had come so far to see the caves. This was like being on holiday. Everybody was friendly, relaxed and prepared to talk.

They had all been to the South; the man from Omagh's wife was a member of the Women's Institute, which had sisterly connections with the Irish Countrywomen's Association, the Woman's Institute being a Protestant organization. The woman from Omagh knew someone who lived near my home town. I told her that my mother was a member of the Irish Countrywomen's Association, and she seemed pleased.

They were all Protestants, and I was delighted with myself that they weren't hostile to my Southern accent, or my sudden arrival. I was sorry I knew nothing about sheep, and was thus prevented from joining in the conversation. I told the couple from Omagh about Lough Melvin and how beautiful it was there, and they were interested in this. The landlady and the woman from Omagh talked about the joys of the microwave oven, as I had my apple pie and cream.

Tea would be served in the other room, or coffee if we preferred, the landlady said. There was a big colour television in the corner. The news was on. The news was bad. A part-time UDR man had been shot dead in Belfast in front of his son. There had been an attempt on the life of a Catholic, but the gun had jammed and the man had miraculously escaped.

'When will the killing ever stop?' asked the landlady's husband.

'Never,' said the man from Omagh, with a sigh. We watched the pictures of the small street where the man was killed, and we heard local people describe how the killers had been able to escape into a Catholic area; later a wall would be put up, separating the Protestants and the Catholics.

The tea came and we turned the television off. We had had enough news for one day. The women talked about food, various ways of cooking and storing food, and we all listened. I had said very little during the evening. I said nothing about the killings in Belfast. I felt a bit funny sitting there, contributing nothing. So when the talk came around to the soup made from beetroot I mentioned that it was called bortsch and was Polish.

'That's right,' the landlady said. For one moment I had the attention of the entire company who smiled at me politely. Without an instant's thought I added: 'The Pope really likes it. He has someone in Rome who makes it for him.'

Everyone looked down. The room echoed with a deep silence. The landlady, the landlady's husband, the man from Omagh and his wife, and the man whose wife wasn't well, paled at the remark. The Pope: I had mentioned the Pope. What sort of fool was I? I was about to apologize for mentioning the name of the Pope and offer to go to bed forthwith and leave them to their own devices, but that would clearly have made things worse. The silence hung on, broken only by the landlady asking if anyone wanted more tea. The man from Omagh and his wife said it was time they went to bed, they had a long day ahead of them; and the man whose wife wasn't well said he was going to bed too. I muttered something myself about going to bed. The landlady removed the cups and saucers and I slipped quietly out of the room.

The breakfast in the morning would have gladdened the heart of even His Holiness, if he ever had occasion to visit Florencecourt. Not only were there rashers, sausages, egg, tomato, but the plate also had fried mushrooms and a potato cake and a soda farl. This was a real Ulster fry. The couple from Omagh departed as I finished, having signed their names in the book. When I retrieved my rucksack and went down to pay, I discovered that the landlady had disappeared, and I paid a girl in the kitchen. The visitors' book was still in the dining room so I went in, ready to sign my name. The couple from Omagh had each signed, giving their full names and address. When it came to nationality, they had both signed themselves British.

I had always known that Protestants in the North considered themselves British, but when I saw it there in fresh biro it came as a shock. They were from Omagh, they talked with Omagh accents. How could they be British? As I walked towards the main road, having signed myself Irish, noticing that the 'Forward to Victory: Join the Ulster Clubs' signs were still on the poles, and that a British army helicopter was flying low overhead, I gave myself a good kick for mentioning the Pope. And another for being surprised at the couple from Omagh signing themselves British.

It was a bright morning. I watched a bunch of crows in a field of bog. The fields were soggy now after the rain, and the farmers were full of despair. I came on to the main road leading South, and met an old man who told me that the sun wouldn't last long, the rain would be down soon. As I ambled along the main road, which was narrow and badly surfaced, the dark clouds appeared once more. There was going to be more rain. Lorries whizzed by.

At the British army border post, a soldier stood with his rifle pointed towards the ground.

'It's bad weather, sir,' he said.

'It's a hard life,' I replied.

'No, it isn't sir,' he laughed with a sort of bitterness. 'No, it isn't, sir.'

There were Irish army jeeps parked outside the Garda station in Swanlinbar. The town consisted of one long street full of public houses, which led to another street where there were more public houses. The Swan Luxury Lounge, Bridge End, Cullen's Bar and Lounge, Breffni Bar. Then six pubs in a row, right beside each other, with no normal domestic relief: Claddagh Lounge, Greyhound Bar, The Welcome Inn, Lounge Bar for Sale, Young's, Talk of the Town. There was also a bar further down called O'Luinigh, and another on the opposite side of the street which had no name, plus another nearer the border called The First And Last. I chanced the Swan Luxury Lounge. For a while I was the only customer, until a farmer came in and ordered a bottle of Guinness. The ensuing conversation concerned the weather, the fact that the fields were soaking wet, and the weather forecast promised more rain. There were farmers up to their necks in debt, he said, from last year. Last year was a disaster; this year was going to be worse, he said. A lot of men were going to be ruined, if the weather didn't improve. The woman behind the bar nodded sympathetically, as did I.

I made my way back up the street in this town of public houses, some of them closed now and a few of them derelict, to The First And Last, which seemed to be the best-kept pub in town, a settee in the corner, nice tables and comfortable chairs, as well as fresh flowers around the room. The woman behind the bar told me that the pub used to do good business at weekends, and that there was a good trade from the North on a Sunday. Now, she said, if they had twelve people it was a good night. Usually they only had about four. The border and rising prices had made the difference. I asked her about the road to Derrylin; she said it was closed to traffic, but thought I could do it on foot.

I went back towards the North that afternoon, not along the main road to Enniskillen, which I had just covered, but in an easterly direction towards Kinawley and Derrylin. I passed a dump full of rusty cans and plastic bags as the road began to peter out.

After the first huge concrete block with the familiar girders sticking up towards the sky, denoting the border, there was no sign that there had been a road, only a tiny pathway, full of mucky puddles, and a stream which I had to jump across, followed by a second concrete blockade, followed by a swamp. The road had been closed for about thirty years, since the IRA border campaign of the 1950s, and now it had gone completely back to nature. Someone had placed fording stones across a second stream, which I crossed when I had made my way along the clumps of vegetation in the swamps. A path led into a field. A few pigeons flew up in the air in agitation at my approach. It was like a scene from a movie where everything is still and calm, until a few birds fly up, and then you know that someone is coming and there will be some action.

There was no action, of course, just the sound of a helicopter in the distance, and the field giving on to a country lane. My map was useless; I swore I would replace it with a detailed Ordnance Survey map as soon as I could. I had to ask a group of children who were playing outside a house for directions to Kinawley.

I stopped at a house and asked an old man who was working in the garden to confirm these directions. It was a bad day, he said; it was a bad summer.

'Do you think it will get any better?' I asked him.

'Do you not think,' he said, his eyes narrowed and staring at me intensely, 'that we'll soon see the end of the world?'

'Why do you think we'll see the end of the world?'

He explained. His mother had heard it from her grandmother; it was always said that the world would end when there were carts without horses, when you would meet six different armies within one mile, when you couldn't tell the difference between a man and a woman, when you couldn't tell the difference between summer and winter. I knew what he meant by three of these, but how were there six armies within one mile? He listed them out: the RUC, the British army, the UDR, the Free State Gardaí, the Free State Army and the water rats.

The water rats? I didn't understand. The water rats, he repeated. The Irish customs officials, he explained.

What happened in Russia, the explosion at Chernobyl, was only the beginning, he said. Soon the world would end. In the meantime, he had decorated his house and had received a grant of £9,300 from the government for the improvements; his son had come home from Birmingham to help. There wasn't much to do around the area, he said, but he rode his bicycle into Kinawley every night for a few drinks in Corrigan's public house.

You seldom saw the army or the police in the area, he said, but when they came, it was like bees out of a hive, swarming around, asking questions. There had been craters blasted into the road originally to block the border, but when the locals filled them in, they put up the concrete blocks.

Suddenly, the wind blew up. The old man looked up at the sky. 'There's going to be rain,' he said. 'You'd know by the wind.' He pointed out the way to Kinawley, which made nonsense of the map, and I told him I might see him later in the pub.

The weather was like an opera, as though the orchestra was slowly building up tension and volume, preparing the audience for a major aria. The sky was darkening, the wind was strong. Just before the downpour I met two young fellows outside a house. When they heard I was from the South, they told me that this was bandit country, and they laughed. No land patrols came along this road, it wasn't safe. This was all Catholic land; it was bad land, divided mostly into thirty-acre holdings; the people lived off grants from the government.

At the weekend they went to dances, mostly in the South, in Carrick-on-Shannon or Mohill, but also sometimes in Omagh. On rainy nights, they said, the army would take you out of the car and make you stand there, delay you, ask you questions, your name, your address, where you were going, where you were coming from; particularly if you were going to a dance and were dressed up. When the army came around, having landed from helicopters, they wanted to know the names of the dogs on each farm, they told me. Imagine, wanting to know the names of the dogs. There was nothing they didn't want to know.

I mentioned the car accidents which had occurred in the area. Both of them looked at me, puzzled, wondering why I had brought this up. I shrugged. No reason, they mentioned dances and driving and it just came into my head. In two years, one of them said, six boys from his class had been killed in different car accidents. There had been other accidents in the area as well, in which more had been killed. They were all Catholics.

'People think it's revenge,' one of them said.

'Revenge?' The rain was starting now, but I couldn't move on, and they didn't want to ask me into the house.

'What do you mean, revenge?' They weren't sure whether to tell me or not, they looked at each other. No, they didn't mean that these young people had been killed deliberately, but the older people said it was because of the Grahams. Had I heard of the Grahams? I had, I said. They were the three brothers who were killed one by one by the IRA, the last while he was waiting to drive a bus full of Catholic children to swim in Enniskillen. Yes, one of them said, the older people maintained that the accidents were a sort of revenge for what was done to the Grahams. God, you know, did I understand? It was God. It seemed like a large number of young people from the same area, I said, to be killed in accidents. They nodded grimly. I said I didn't think it was God. No, they agreed, they didn't either. It was just something which was said.

'Will things ever change?' one of them asked me. The question was earnest, and they looked at me as though I should know.

'I don't know,' I answered.

The rain came down hard. I was soaking wet by the time I got to Kinawley. I was dripping with rain as I walked into Corrigan's pub. My feet were sore and I was fed up. I was having a drink as the evening news came on. The IRA were promising to shoot anyone who collaborated in any way with the security forces, including those who worked at the building of RUC stations, or who delivered to these stations.

The RUC barracks in Kinawley, next door to Corrigan's, had been bombed again and again by the IRA. On several occasions the windows of the local Catholic church had been shattered in the blast; at one stage the roof had been blown off the side aisle of the church. Then, in 1978 a lorry was hijacked by the IRA and parked in the grounds of the church; it was used as the base for a rocket attack, and a whole side of the barracks was demolished and had since been re-built.

Most of the personnel and supplies came to the barracks by helicopter. Its proximity to the pub meant that drinking had to conclude at the appointed time. No army or police would be served in the pub, whose clientele were all nationalists.

The rain now looked as though it was down for the night. The nearest place to stay was Derrylin, about four miles away. I didn't fancy walking any further. I had another drink and considered my position. I imagined the hotel room, the bar of the hotel, the sort of dinner I would get, the long march in the rain, an hour's walk. I shuddered. Something snapped. I revolted. I went to the telephone and dialled Basil Lenaghan's number. I had told him in Ballyshannon that I would call him. Here I was. I explained my plight. When he laughed, his laugh was as loud as it had been in Ballyshannon. He told me to stay where I was, have another drink, he would come and collect me in his car. There was a spare bed, he said. Good.

When he arrived, he was in full flight, immediately getting involved with a few local men up at the bar on the issue of whether the Gaelic Athletic Association should let their precious playing fields be used for soccer, which they refused to do. Basil insisted that they were wrong. The men at the bar eyed him suspiciously.

'Soccer is an English game,' one of them said. There was no further discussion.

We stopped at the off-licence at Blake's in Derrylin, which was a relation of Blake's in Enniskillen, where I went to buy a bottle of wine. 'Do you know about wines?' the young fellow asked me in a rich Fermanagh accent. When I didn't reply, he brought me on a tour of the French reds, explaining the temper and flavour of each one. I bought a good bottle at less than half the price it would have cost me in the South.

There was a big fire lighting in the living room of Basil's bungalow; his wife Joanne was there and his little daughter Clare. Basil filled me a Black Bush.

Dinner was ready: new potatoes from the garden, quiche, a green bean salad with garlic dressing, followed by cheese. The wind was roaring up the hill from Lough Erne, the rain still pouring down. I was glad to be inside.

Later Basil, who worked in the Forestry Service, and myself, in typical male tradition, went out for a drink, running from the front door of the house to the car to avoid the rain. He drove into Brookeborough. He told me how he was stopped once by a

UDR patrol, who asked him the usual questions. A mile later, he was stopped by another UDR patrol, who seemed set to start him all over again about his name, address, destination, and business. He told them he had just answered the same questions a few minutes previously only to be met with a scream from the head of the patrol, instructing him to get out of the car and ordering him to answer the questions again. He did.

We went into Healy's pub beside the Orange Hall in Brookeborough, which was sporting a Union Jack. There were a few men up at the bar. Forestry was a sensitive issue in Fermanagh as well as Leitrim. The most suitable land for clearance was poor land, which was mainly in Catholic hands. The ownership of land was a deeply emotional issue, and the talk in the pub hovered around it for some time.

A man told me that the fourth Graham, whose three brothers had been shot by the IRA, often came into the pub. He wasn't in the UDR, unlike his three brothers, and he was popular in the area, the man said. A few weeks previously he had been standing in the corner of the bar with a drink in his hand, when someone had said to him as a joke, as a throwaway line, something like: 'If you don't finish that drink I'll kill you.' He heard the fourth Graham brother answer: 'Sure you've killed my three brothers, you might as well kill me.'

★

It was raining so hard the next morning I could barely see Lough Erne from Basil's front window. I stayed in bed late, afraid to face the day. After breakfast, I sat in the living room playing records, wondering if there was any point in going out at all. Lunch went by, and I still hadn't moved. It was only when Basil offered to drive me as far as Lisnaskea that I picked up my rucksack and walked to the car.

At Lisnaskea, I got a lift to Derrylin. There was hardly any colour at all in this world. The sky hung low over us, and when we crossed the Erne over a low metal bridge the water was a dull grey as well. The road had started to flood; if the rain kept up, the driver said, it would soon be impassable.

Derrylin today bore no resemblance to Derrylin that Sunday

when we went to drink in the hotel after a day on the boat. It was dreary now, the rain hopping off the street, the main street desolate in the rain. I walked right up to the top of the town, and knocked on the door of the priest's house. The priest, Father Gaffney, was just finishing his supper. I asked him about the killing by the IRA of James Graham, the third brother.

It happened, he told me, in February of the previous year. He was across the road in the graveyard with a man whose father had died. They were looking at plots when he heard the firing. Graham was in his bus waiting for the children to take them to the swimming pool. It was before ten. Graham, who was a part-time UDR man, had already done his normal run with the school bus; this was a special run.

Father Gaffney heard them shoot in the air as they escaped in a van, and they shouted as though it was a great victory, he said. The van was later found up in the mountains.

Father Gaffney and his curate, Michael Harding, issued a statement condemning the killing. They went to the funeral service in a small country church. They wore their collars. The church was packed; they stood outside. A few times they noticed people pointing at them and whispering. The Church of Ireland bishop, who had preached to the congregation about forgiveness, came over and thanked them for coming. There was a UDR guard of honour, and a piper led the coffin into the graveyard before the Last Post was played.

The Bishop was grateful for their presence. There were others, however, who saw it as an affront. Over the next month a fierce controversy raged between the two priests and a Presbyterian minister over the attitude of the Catholic church to violence. In public statement after counter-statement, the clergy debated the issue. It was bitter.

I met Michael Harding, the curate in Derrylin, in Dublin once. I asked him about the shouts for joy that Father Gaffney had heard, the whoops which he had told me that the IRA had given as they escaped after killing James Graham. Had he heard them too? He had been standing at the door of the Presbytery, he said. Yes, he had heard them. What did they sound like? I

wanted to know. It was a wild howl, he said. Yes, but what exactly
did it sound like? He did it for me in a high-pitched voice.

'Ya-hoo, ya-hoo, ya-hoo,' they screamed when they killed the
third Graham brother.

7

Hard Rain, Thatcherism and the Protestant Inheritance

I set off from Derrylin to walk to Ballyconnell. The rain came down in torrents. The road was narrow, and passing cars splashed water all over me. I was disconsolate, sorry I hadn't stayed with Basil and Joanne, oozing self-pity. Sometimes the rain would ease off and then start up again with immense ferocity, as though it was playing cat and mouse with the world. My shoes were now letting in the wet. Although it was only seven o'clock, signs of night were apparent. This was miserable.

At one point the road was blocked with floods, and I had to edge my way along the middle rung of a wooden fence, since the road was under at least a foot of water. There was a bridge over a narrow stream, which was now carrying tons of muddy water with immense speed. It was as though the winter had suddenly returned or the great flood, and the road to Ballyconnell was endless. Up hill, down hill, bends in the road, straight stretches in the road, rain everywhere, soggy fields, rain running along the road as if the road was a river bed, cars splashing muck and muddy water all over. Me walking.

Eventually, I came to a cement factory, with lorries bearing the name 'Sean Quinn' parked in the yard. The factory, its offices, quarries and outhouses went on for about a mile. And after them was an army post, with a dry soldier wanting to know where I was coming from and where I was going.

If I expected to find Ballyconnell just beyond the army post, just over the border, I was wrong. It was another half an hour of sheer pain before I walked into the town and found myself a bed for the night. I put my clothes on a heater with my poor shoes beside them and got into bed. By the time I woke up they were almost dry, and it was time to venture out to explore the night life of Ballyconnell.

There was a young girl behind the bar of the Angler's Rest who talked to the couple and two young fellows who sat at the bar. She was emigrating, she said, there was nothing for her to do here. Everyone was going now. She was going to London. She'd never find a job in Ireland, she said. The other girl said she had been to New York to see her brother. He wanted to come home on holiday, but he couldn't, since, like a hundred thousand other young Irish people, he was an illegal immigrant in the United States; once he left, he wouldn't be able to go back. The two fellows at the bar talked about leaving as well. New York was the place to go; there was always work there, they said.

The recent census figures had shown that emigration, which had solved the unemployment problem of the 1940s and 1950s when people left the Republic to work in England and America, had returned. Between April 1985 and April 1986 the net emigration figure from the Republic was thirty-one thousand; most of these people had left Ireland to find work. Most of them were young, and many of them well educated. The newspapers carried reports of football teams in villages losing half their members in one year through emigration.

Yet Ballyconnell was lucky; Sean Quinn's quarry was just up the road and there was a plastics factory in the town. In other towns there was nothing. But even here there wasn't enough to keep young people from leaving.

There was a bigger crowd up the street that night in the Crow's Nest. When it came to closing time I discovered that the Gardaí in Ballyconnell were not vigilant about drinking hours, I waited for the lights to be turned down and time to be called. Instead, more drink was poured. The man beside me owned a petrol station in the town. I offered him my sympathy; he told me that a roaring trade was being done by the petrol station which was north of the border, but on the southern side of the army checkpoint. He didn't do so badly, however, he said. The Gardaí, the Irish army and all the public servants used his station. We ordered our last drink at twelve-thirty, and everyone was still drinking happily as I wandered home fifteen minutes later. The following morning I awoke from uneasy dreams and turned on the radio. There was big news about the border. I thought of going to the window and checking if it was all happening on the streets of Ballyconnell, but when the headlines were repeated I knew that I was miles away from the action.

The action had been caused by Peter Robinson, the deputy leader of the Democratic Unionist Party, while his leader Ian Paisley was in America. He had gathered together his followers, a chosen people, and marched on the South where they had scrawled slogans on the walls of the village of Clontibret, beaten up two Gardaí, and made general nuisances of themselves. The purpose of this raid in the early hours of the morning was to show that there was no border security, that if a group of diehard Unionists could travel freely across the border, then what could a small, stealthy band of IRA men do? Peter Robinson was arrested.

*

When I got up, I rang Sean Quinn, the quarry owner whose name was on most of the lorries in this locality, and he agreed to see me in the afternoon. Several of his green lorries passed me as I walked back towards the North. At the border the bloke from the army ascertained that I was walking. 'Rather you than me,' he said.

At the first office I was told that Sean Quinn was to be found in another building up the road. I kept walking. It was another dark, dreary day, but there was no rain.

Sean Quinn conformed, here in bandit country, where the UDR foot patrols were afraid to venture, to a Thatcherite blueprint. When I arrived at his office I had to wait. His assistant came in to fill me in on the background. Sean Quinn had inherited a twenty-three acre farm in 1973; he was now a millionaire. He had begun to deliver gravel, then diversified into concrete blocks and tiles. His enterprise had grown every year. He had benefited enormously from the early years of Thatcher, when there was a hundred per cent, tax-free allowance on profits which were re-invested. There were no trade unions in his business, nor was any employee paid a salary. Everyone was paid according to productivity.

His fame had spread far and wide, not just as an employer, a success story and a name over lorries, but as a man who hit a British soldier at a checkpoint, knocked him over and drove on. The soldier was black, according to some in the pub the previous night. Everyone agreed that there had been no retaliation. He was too important, Sean Quinn.

I asked Sean Quinn's assistant about relations with the army. 'There is generally no problem,' he said, 'just when a new regiment comes, it takes time to get used to them'. He didn't mention his boss hitting a soldier. Sixty per cent of the business was in the South, he continued, and there was a special agreement with the Northern customs people that the export documents were handed in at the Southern office and sent North, in one of those informal arrangements. Forty per cent of the staff of the 140 came from the South. Certain things were cheaper in the South, he said, lorry tyres, for example, and road tax.

Eventually, the great Thatcherite himself came in. He was a dark, good-looking, gruff man in his late thirties, wearing an old grey pullover. He talked with an off-hand precision; the accent was straight Fermanagh. We were interrupted a few times by lorry drivers, who wanted to ask him something, and he seemed as at ease as they seemed diffident. He didn't act like the boss. And he certainly didn't look like a millionaire.

His father willed him this small farm, he told me. He had left school when he was young; he wasn't interested in it, unlike his brother and sisters. He was interested in making money and having a good time. He was known all over Fermanagh, Catholic Fermanagh, because he had been captain of the Gaelic football team in the early seventies, so when he advertised the gravel, undercutting other suppliers, people trusted him, liked him, wanted to do business with him. Things grew from there. Thatcher, he agreed, had improved the climate for business when she came to power, but in the past few years she had started to reduce incentives for investment.

Sean Quinn's big plan for expansion was being put into place down the road. He was spending twenty-five million pounds on a new cement factory, which would supply twenty-two per cent of the market, North and South. How did the present suppliers view his plans? I asked. 'They are not overjoyed,' he said.

The phone on his desk rang. He picked it up and began a long conversation with a man who had a strong British accent. He had a notebook on his desk and he began to write down figures, issuing instructions about buying and selling. I couldn't work out what he was doing. He was dour and casual, ringing off without any salutation, and trying to pick up the thread of what we were saying when the phone rang.

I interrupted him to ask what he was talking about on the phone. Stocks and shares, he said. He had started, six months before, to play the stock market. He showed me the list of items he dealt in – gold, oil, the Swiss franc against the dollar, aluminium. His broker, he said, phoned twice or three times a day and he told him what to do. A salesman brought him out the *Financial Times* from Enniskillen, so that he could read about his investments. It was interesting, he said, suggesting that playing the stock market was a form of amusement, implying somehow that it was a common pastime around Derrylin and Teemore.

He responded immediately when I asked him if he had floored a British soldier at the border. He did, he said. The British army post had been put up three years before. His lorries went through one hundred and fifty times a day, and each time they were delayed for an average of two minutes. I could, he looked at me sternly, calculate the cost myself. It was more or less the same as keeping one lorry full-time on the road, I said. He nodded. Why did he hit the soldier? I asked. He was going to a funeral, he said, and he was already late. They stopped him at the border, made him drive into the side and held him there, even though he passed up and down several times a day, even though his name was written on each of the 150 lorries which passed through the checkpoint. Time passed. They wouldn't let him go. After half an hour he told the soldier that he was going anyway, whether the soldier agreed or not. He knocked the soldier over and drove off.

I asked him about the IRA's threat to builders and suppliers who had dealings with the British army. He said that a friend of his had been shot dead by the IRA for doing business with the

security forces, but that he himself didn't supply the security forces
or deal with them, and never had; he was a nationalist. 'I didn't
think it was prudent,' he said. He employed a few Protestants, he
said, but there weren't very many in the area.

He lived just over the border in the South on the road between
Ballyconnell and Belturbet. He had bought land in the South,
land his father had owned in the 1950s, land he remembered
going to look at on an ass and cart, which he now drove to in
his Mercedes. Land wasn't a good investment, he said, but he
enjoyed going to look at stock two or three evenings a week. He
was careful to avoid buying small pieces of land or pubs in the
area and depriving local people of the chance to buy and make
their sole living from them. Instead, he had bought the Cat and
Cage pub in Drumcondra in Dublin for £640,000. He leased it
out, but had recently enjoyed having a drink there after a football
match in Dublin where he was following the fortunes of the
Tyrone team.

He drove me to the border in his big car. He seemed genuinely
puzzled by my walking. 'Can you not afford to buy a car?' he
asked. He seemed to be expressing concern about my welfare.
The soldier at the checkpoint waved him on. I told him what I
had heard: that in the days following his assault on the soldier,
they had carried truncheons, according to the people I spoke to
in Ballyconnell. He chuckled to himself about this. We passed the
filling station, still in the North, and it was doing thriving business.
As we came to the line which separated the North from the
South, County Fermanagh from County Cavan, he let me out,
told me the story of the house which the border went right
through like a slicer through a block of cheese, and drove off.

The house was a small, modest, old-fashioned cottage. When
I knocked on the door a man in his sixties came out. His name
was Felix Murray, I discovered, and the border ran through his
house in which he and his two brothers lived. These days, he
said, all three slept in the North, but there was a time when one
of them had slept in the South. 'Only an odd time now,' he said,
'we sleep in the State'. There was a sofa in the kitchen, he pointed
out through the window, where you could sit and let the border
run through you.

They got their dog licence in the South, he said, it was cheaper, but their television licence, on the other hand, they bought in the North where it cost less. Their electricity was connected in the South, but their water in the North. They voted in the North. The grants were better in the North, he said. The border checkpoint was a nuisance, he said. Recently when he was crossing from North to South on his bicycle he passed a red light, which called for the driver to stop, only to be told by the soldier that this applied to bicycles as well.

He changed the subject back to his predicament. He seemed to have it off by heart and it disturbed him that he had omitted a detail. Yes, he remembered, the postman came every day, one from the North and one from the South. The southern one came earlier.

I sympathized with him for the inconvenience of living in two states. He said it wasn't too bad; that wasn't the worst part of it at all. What was the worst part of it? I asked. He looked across the road to the ditch and the hill beyond the ditch. He left a dramatic silence. The interviewers, he said, the reporters, the television cameras; since he was a child they had come to tell the story of the Murrays cut in two by the border. There wasn't a single day went by but there wasn't a knock at the door. Yesterday a bus pulled up outside and he had 'seen them all leppin' out and taking snaps'.

People had come 'from America and all over' to see the house. They never had any peace, himself or his brothers. That was the worst thing, he said, and looked at me frankly. I understood, I said. I took his point. He went back into the house and I walked back towards Ballyconnell.

As I made my way along, a huge car stopped and a man with a British accent offered me a lift. He said he was going to Belturbet, which was where I was going. I thought it would be churlish to refuse. The weather was still nasty-looking. I told him I had been talking to the big man himself, Sean Quinn. Yes, he said, he worked for Sean Quinn; he was in charge of getting the cement factory built in time and within budget. He had been a salesman, he said, and Quinn had spotted him and offered him the job.

We passed by Sean Quinn's house on the right-hand side of the road. It was much more modest than I had expected. We drove on to a side road and went along by a lake. The driver liked it around here, he said, it was beautiful; he liked Sean Quinn, liked the locals. He stopped at a junction and turned left. This was once the main Dublin to Enniskillen road, he said, now it was like a lane, leading nowhere; the bridge between the North and the South had been blown up.

There were still two houses on the southern side of the blown-up bridge. A few kids played in front of them as we got out of the car to look at the remains of the bridge. It had been a beautiful old stone bridge, we could still see bits of the stone, like innards, on the opposite side. It was hard not to feel an intense regret that it had not been spiked, or blocked; blowing it up, blowing away all the soft-coloured cut stone, seemed a travesty.

We drove into Belturbet and had several drinks in the Diamond Bar. The bar on the opposite side of the square was called the Railway Bar, but there was no railway here anywhere, just as there was no direct contact with the North. I went in search of a bed for the night as my driver went home for his dinner. I left my rucksack in a bed and breakfast, told the landlady that I wanted to be up early in the morning, found a bite to eat, and returned to the Diamond Bar. I sat up on a high stool and watched the first batch of lorries coming through the Diamond outside, travelling from the South with hay for the stricken farmers of the North, who had been ruined by the weather. For weeks now these lorries would be a constant presence on the roads.

They had opened the bridge one year, they told me in the bar; they had built a sort of temporary bridge at Christmas in 1972. And that was how the bombers made their way into Belturbet from the North and planted a bomb in the Diamond outside, just after Christmas in the same year. They pointed to the stool I was sitting on: the bomb had blown a man sitting on that stool over the counter, it had blown the door in. No one in the bar had died, but two people out in the Diamond had been killed, including a youth who was in the telephone box making a call. One of the Protestant paramilitary groups had carried out the bombing. The bridge hadn't been opened since.

The radio in the bar was tuned into a local illegal station, whose headquarters were a few miles down the road, which played country and western music all day and all night. It could be heard as far North as Strabane. It carried advertisements from almost every town within fifty miles. The American country and western stars joined in with their Irish counterparts in pulling the heartstrings of the locality where country and western music was big business. Johnny Cash sang 'O Lonesome Me' to be followed by a local singer, Big Tom, who sang 'Will I Ne'er See You More, Gentle Mother?' The next song was called 'Diane, If You're Going To Do Wrong Again, You Might As Well Do Wrong Again With Me'. I went home.

In the morning over breakfast the landlady asked me where I was from. I told her I was from Wexford; she said it was one of the two counties in Ireland where she had never been. Why was she so well travelled? I asked. Weddings, she said, she used to go to a lot of weddings. Now she didn't go to any. At one time, she explained, there were fourteen Gardaí staying in this house. It was the mid-seventies, when border security was being stepped up, and the hunt for IRA men was being conducted with great enthusiasm. All the Gardaí were young; the force was full of new recruits. They were all single, and all the men stationed in Belturbet and environs stayed with her, which was why I might have noticed that there were three beds in my room. She had filled the house with beds; the Gardaí had come and gone at all hours of the day and night. But in subsequent years they had decided, as all young healthy Gardaí would, to get married. And they had, being well mannered, and being grateful to their former landlady for the big fry-ups in the morning, the motherly chats and the clean sheets, invited her to their weddings in every part of Ireland, except Wexford and one other county, Waterford. So the Gardaí were all gone from her now, like the poor woman Maurya in Synge's *Riders to the Sea*, except for one solitary Garda who still remained, like the drunk at the wedding, after all the others had departed. She looked at me wistfully. She missed them, she said.

I asked her about the bomb in 1972. She was at home, at the time, she said. She had heard it. It had damaged a great number of the houses around, but many people did not notice the damage until several years later, when the roof began to sag, or walls started to crack, and it was too late to apply for compensation.

I paid her and went back up for a final drink in the Diamond Bar. An English family who, it emerged, came every year for the fishing, were there to say goodbye. They'd had a wonderful holiday, they said, and they would of course be back next year. The front bar was a pleasure, each bottle at the bar gleaming in the morning light; the wooden counter was well polished, the radio playing country and western.

When I walked down the hill towards the river, I could see the last navigation marks for boats travelling on Lough Erne. It was possible to sail from here as far as Belleek, crossing the border twice. The water was quiet this morning under the cloudy sky with patches of blue sky appearing and being covered again with clouds. I was almost knocked down by a speeding red car as I went towards Wattlebridge in the North.

Rain had now begun, black clouds having drawn in out of nowhere. I passed over the river Finn once more, which was brown in colour and seemed to wend its mellow way around the Cavan–Fermanagh border with no great sense of urgency.

The rain was getting harder. There was a large tear in my plastic mac, and the rain was getting through and wetting my pullover. I stopped at a shop and petrol station and bought a bar of chocolate. When I stood outside under the shelter of the roof of the petrol station, the woman who ran the place came out and looked at me maliciously, as though I was causing some sort of obstruction, as though I was Peter Robinson. I glared back at her, but eventually grew tired making a nuisance of myself and moved on, mine not to reason why, into the downpour.

The ditches were so full of fertility that mushrooms were rampant. I was watching for the border and looking at a map of Ireland; I noticed a little thumb sticking up from the South into the North, making the map look silly; it seemed as though you couldn't even walk into this thumb, let alone drive a car, but this tiny stretch of land, the sort of territory that only Fortinbras himself would bother trying to capture, belonged to the Republic of Ireland and not Her Majesty the Queen. There was no divorce in this thumb; what God had put together, let no man tear asunder in this thumb. Petrol and drink were expensive in this small phallic incursion into the North.

I walked into the green freedom of the South once I had passed an X-sign for helicopters; it didn't feel any different, and the rain was the same. I went by a ruined church and a bricked-up building, which might once have been a school. The sun came out, but the rain didn't stop. I met a young fellow outside a house who gave me careful directions to Scotshouse in County Monaghan. I was to turn right, then left, then across a bridge and take the next right and when I came to the river again I was to turn right again. His father came out and repeated the instructions. This inspired confidence, so I decided to take their word for it and go to Scotshouse, rather than Clones.

By the time I found the first turn to the right the full arc of a rainbow had appeared across the sky, starting way up in the North and projecting far down into the South. And when a second rainbow started it was even better. The sun came out again, but the rain poured down with an even greater intensity, and it was getting into my shoes. It was all too much for me, and I prayed for dullness, the old grey sky I had become used to.

The rain softened, started up again, softened and erupted once more as though someone had pulled a spring back and let it loose. The legs of my trousers below the plastic mac were now drenched and the tear in the mac was letting in gallons of water. I was used to watching rain from a refined distance, from the window of a house, or a bus, from the back seat of a taxi, from the window of a public house. I wasn't used to this exposure. I seemed to be passing over and over from the North into the South, the South into the North, walking down through this thumb, which I had jeered for its inconsequence, its puniness. Now it was getting me back.

I passed once more over the river Finn. Sweet Finn run softly till I get to Scotshouse. When it seemed the rain could not possibly get any harder, it began to pour down even more, wetting me to the bone. There wasn't even a decent tree to shelter under; the place was full of nasty little bushes, thorn trees and grubby briar. The rain was almighty. God himself, it was clear, was conducting the orchestra. I passed by more X-marks for the British army helicopters, but I had no idea whether I was walking into the North or into the South.

Eventually, I came out onto a busier road, where I stopped a fellow on a motorbike and asked him the way to Scotshouse. I turned right and walked on through the hard rain, meeting no traffic except a man leading a few cows, until I came into Scotshouse itself, where I fell into a public house, took off my shoes and socks and sat at the bar in my bare feet.

I knew the Tyrone Guthrie Centre was just a few miles away, and I knew I was done walking for some time. I rang Bernard Loughlin, told him where I was, explained myself, and slyly suggested that if he had nothing better to do, he might come over and collect me. He said he'd be over in a few minutes, and I rested in peace, a pint of beer in my poor wet hand.

I wasn't long at Bernard's house, however, until I was wearing dry socks, clean underwear and dry clothes. I was my old self again. I was full of the fact that I had rung Lord Brookeborough's grandson, Alan Brooke, from Belturbet, and his wife had seemed rather sympathetic to the idea that I might wander up and see him. I rang again from Bernard's house and spoke to the man himself, who within a year would inherit the title on his father's death. I could come the following Monday, he said, for soup. He specified soup. If I came at one o'clock I could have 'soup' with them. He seemed like a nice fellow on the telephone, but I couldn't work out as he spoke whether he was joking about 'soup'. The aristocracy were getting ironic in these difficult times, I thought, and surely old Lord Brookeborough's grandson and the then Lord Brookeborough's son, was capable of a joke.

It was a pretty good joke. I told it to several people around the Tyrone Guthrie Centre, who thought it was a good joke too. 'Soup' was what the brethren of the Reformed Churches had offered Catholics during the Famine in return for conversion. Give up all that Roman nonsense, they said, and we'll give you soup. 'Taking the soup' meant going over to the other side. It was still a potent phrase in the country, a regular jibe. To be offered soup by the grandson of Lord Brookeborough was a rare temptation. He couldn't be serious. I looked forward to meeting him.

And that wasn't the only reason. Alan Brooke had caused a huge row in Fermanagh when Sinn Fein and the SDLP, with their new nationalist majority, had withdrawn the grant from a local horse-jumping event with which Alan Brooke was associated. He approached Paul Corrigan of Sinn Fein, Chairman of the Council, and explained to him that this jumping show was an all-Ireland affair, the winner would jump at the Dublin Horse Show. Sinn Fein relented, and Alan Brooke had his grant. Sinn Fein, however, released details of their meeting with Alan Brooke, which caused consternation among the Unionist population who viewed the appeal by Lord Brookeborough's grandson to Sinn Fein with alarm. It wouldn't have happened in the old days.

Alan Brooke had given me precise instructions on how to get to his house, Colebrooke, as opposed to his father's house, Ashbrooke. I convinced Bernard Loughlin to drop me there on his way to Enniskillen the following Monday. We wondered what sort of soup would be on offer.

The man who came out to greet me was not the sort I expected. He didn't smile; there was no ironic curl of the lip, no aristocratic languor about him. He was serious, alert and forthright as he ushered me into the house while Bernard drove away.

'I'm afraid there *is* just soup,' he said.

'That's wonderful,' I said. I was just a little intimidated.

The house was big, built in dull stone. It had been the home of old Lord Brookeborough, Prime Minister of Northern Ireland from 1943 to 1963, Alan's grandfather. Most of the contents were sold on the old Lord's death to pay the huge death duties, but Alan proudly displayed a piece of furniture in the big bare hall, which he had managed to buy back recently. The house had lain empty for several years; now he was glad to be back. He thought the Anglo-Irish Agreement should be scrapped, but he didn't want to talk about politics. The family, at one stage in its history, had farmed twenty-nine thousand acres. Most of this was now gone, and most of what was left was leased out to local farmers; the family still retained about forty acres. They would like to get more back, Alan said, but the leasing system made it difficult. In the winter, he said, he took German tourists hunting in the woods nearby, but now he spent his time attending to the farm.

His wife came with the soup, which was of the fresh tomato variety; there was also toast. I talked about where I had been along the border. They both seemed serious and intense. They lived in a very small part of the house, the kind of quarters in a Big House which Desmond Leslie later described to me as 'a life module'; the rest of it was too difficult to heat. Alan said that he remembered his grandfather with great affection. I asked him about his grandfather's speech on the Twelfth of July in 1933 advising people not to employ Catholics. Alan seemed surprised about the speech, and was sure that his grandfather had been quoted incorrectly and out of context. He had been in Ballinamallard for the Twelfth and had enjoyed it as much as I had.

Alan was worried about a Labour government in Britain, even though the Tories had introduced the Anglo-Irish Agreement. He preferred the Tories. He was fishing on Lough Melvin recently, and had met a Catholic who didn't like the Agreement either, he said. He felt that there was very little support for the Agreement. He felt that the terrorists should be treated more harshly when they were caught.

I told the Brookes that I had been in Hillsborough on the day of the Agreement. When I went out to watch the protest, having eaten an excellent stew in the Castle, I heard Ian Paisley thank the Dowager Lady Brookeborough for attending the protest. I had marvelled to myself that such an august figure in the Unionist world picture could be outside in the November cold while I was inside partaking of stew, but I didn't tell the Brookes that. Alan was surprised when I said his grandmother was outside; his grandmother was dead, he said. I repeated that Paisley had said 'Dowager Lady Brookeborough'. But that wasn't his grandmother, he said. It was his grandfather's second wife. She might have been at the protest. His grandfather had married a second time, for company, he said. I could hear the strong disapproval in his voice at a member of his family, the Unionist aristocracy, being involved in a Paisleyite protest.

The phone rang and he spoke for some time to someone from the BBC who wanted to use a cottage on the estate for a film of

a John McGahern play. It struck me that the Brookeborough
enterprise was almost a parody of its former self: the woods used
by German tourists in the winter, led by the Lord's own son; the
cottage used by the BBC for a film; the big house empty and
unheatable; the land-holding reduced to forty acres; the dowager
attending protest meetings.

He offered to drive me to the village in his jeep. I thanked
his wife for the soup. We drove down the long avenue away from
the house, past the small church which still stood inside the walls
of the Brooke estate, and on to the main road. His father's house
was further along. He told me that Garret FitzGerald had stayed
with his father just before he became Taoiseach. His family, he
said, had first come to Donegal in the sixteenth century, at a time
when Irish landlords were just as harsh as the English ones. I told
him, breaking the silence which had fallen in the jeep, that I was
worried about walking at night. He told me that this was rubbish,
that I had nothing to be afraid of. I told him I was afraid of the
UDR. He said I had no reason to be afraid of them.

As I prepared to get out of the jeep, much chastened by the
soup and conversation, Alan turned to me and told me to be
careful what I wrote. I should take care, he said, to write that
very few people were involved in what was happening in the
North, very few Protestants and very few Catholics, the rest got
on with their lives, he said. I should write that. I thanked him
instead for talking to me and made my way back to County
Monaghan.

*

On the way through Scotshouse in the downpour, I had passed
by a walled estate called Hilton Park, the seat since the early
eighteenth century of the Madden family. The house was now
open to the public as a family hotel, complete with gourmet
food, four-poster beds and a sense of how the other half lives.
Having stayed a few days at the Tyrone Guthrie Centre, I repaired
to Hilton Park in a taxi, being met at the door by Johnny Madden,
the current owner, who had come back to live here with his wife
Lucy and three children.

There were other guests, he said; the four-poster beds were

all full. He seemed very sorry about this, and showed me to a room with a huge double bed and a window looking on to the front lawn and the oak trees, the acorns for which were brought to Hilton Park by one of his ancestors on the occasion of her wedding. He pointed through one of the back windows of the house to the border which lay just behind the house. The house had been enlarged over the centuries; so it was not a good example of any particular type of architecture, but it was big, imposing and extremely comfortable.

There was a huge fire lighting in the drawing room; the other guests were sitting around with drinks in their hands. Johnny Madden seemed somewhat embarrassed as he asked me to write down on a slip of paper the number of drinks I had. He was a farmer and this 'doing Basil', as he put it, didn't come naturally. He didn't mind looking after guests, he said, although he would resent carrying bags upstairs like a butler. Over the next two days he would constantly enquire after my comfort, like Mephistopheles urging on some Faust, whose only wish was to live like a squire, to greater indulgence in food, drink, heat and country air.

He joined his five guests for the dinner which Lucy had cooked. The main course was lamb in a prune sauce; the potatoes were perfectly roasted. There was a big, luscious chocolate pie for dessert, followed by home-made cheese and coffee.

Johnny was chairman of the Clones Annual Show, which was to take place two days later; and he was worried about the weather. There was a time when the Protestant farmers came from the North, as the showground was right on the border, but this had stopped since the killings had started.

He had joined Fine Gael, Garret FitzGerald's party, which went through a liberal phase in the early 1980s, particularly in relation to social issues such as contraception and divorce. For many years a Protestant had sat in the Dáil representing Monaghan, but this was no longer the case. Johnny was bitterly disappointed by the results of the divorce referendum, which he saw as another message from the majority to the Protestant minority. He had made an effort since he came back to Hilton Park to become involved in the society of the South, not just by joining Fine Gael, but by sending his son to the local national school, in

the village of Scotshouse at the gates of the estate, and not to a
Protestant school. He wondered now if there was any future
for Protestants in the Republic. In 1981 Garret FitzGerald had
announced a constitutional crusade to make the South a more
open and pluralist society, but the divorce referendum had ruined
any hope that something serious might emerge from this.

After dinner we repaired to the lounge, where I talked to an
English couple for a while. They seemed to know Ireland, and
when the man spoke he used a Gaelic phrase; his pronunciation
was good. He had studied at the New University of Ulster, and
while there had gone to Donegal on his own initiative to study
Irish, which he spoke fluently. I had never heard an Englishman
speaking Irish before.

The wind whistled outside next morning, and the rain spat
against the big windows. Clones Annual Show had been cancelled;
Johnny and Lucy were going to be busy all day in Clones. Lucy,
however, cooked a sensational breakfast before she left, with a
silver rack on the table where I could place my *Irish Times*. She
asked me what sort of tea I wanted, and mentioned several. I
nodded my head at the last of these, knowing nothing about tea.
I was in a breakfast room at the bottom of the house. The room
was heated by a big stove. The orange juice was fresh.

The weather deteriorated steadily. There was no point in going
out. I had the house to myself now; cheese and fruit had been
left for lunch; I rummaged around and found a full year's edition
of the *New York Times Book Review*; I also found a stereo cassette
player and full-length version of Beethoven's *Fidelio*. I sat on a
long and comfortable sofa; the heat was turned on high, as was
the stereo. I nibbled at cheese, grapes and oranges and flicked
through the book reviews of a whole year, some of them full of
deep malice, others bland and benign, some of them demon-
strating the reviewer's ignorance, others showing the reviewer's
superior knowledge and writing style. I picked up a great deal of
useful information about such matters as the South American
novel, the decline of the West, the growth of big business and
the private lives of famous writers: the stuff book reviews are
made of. I grew fat with cheese and knowledge, waiting for the

devil himself to knock at the door and declare that my time was up, I was his now, I was his.

The devil, however, was busy elsewhere. The bad weather became a storm, became a hurricane, became Hurricane Charlie. All over Ireland, trees fell down, roads were flooded. In the south-west, whole towns were flooded, as were parts of Dublin. As the day went on I knew how lucky I was to be at Hilton Park, and not on the side of the road, or in some awful bed and breakfast joint.

The spectre of John Madden, great-grandfather of my host, haunted the house. He had left diaries behind, with entries for every day, and regular reports of his bank balance. They were stacked in a metal box in the corner of the breakfast room. Old John Madden had strong opinions on the rights of landlords and the duties of government to uphold those rights. When he added the frontage to the house, he included steel shutters on each window of the ground floor, with a small hinged opening in each one so that a rifle could be directed at any horde which might gather outside.

When I tired of the book reviewers I directed my attention to John Madden's doings. Many of his diary pages resembled those of poor Mr Pooter in *Diary of a Nobody* – ordinary, everyday occurrences in the life of a man of a certain standing, slightly pompous, somewhat snobbish. While the accounts of his bank balance, or of his wife's health, became tedious, his comments on the natives and their antics were highly interesting. He noted that the 'papists' in Scotshouse had been involved in vicious faction fighting after a football match. He was delighted at the fall of Parnell. After the name Mrs O'Shea, he placed the words 'God Bless Her', presumably for her part in bringing down the leader of the Irish Parliamentary Party, and therefore scuppering the prospect of Home Rule in 1891.

John Madden of Hilton Park, the diarist and man of steel shutters, had been involved in considerable controversy in 1869 and 1870 when he was appointed High Sheriff for County Leitrim, along with his other public duties. He wrote to Dublin Castle, seat of the British administration in Ireland, to admonish the government for conducting 'the affairs of my unhappy country in such a way that in less than a year we have been reduced from a state of comparative prosperity to a condition when law, order and security for either life or property may be said to have practically ceased to exist, and the very fabric of society itself seems threatened with dissolution'. The Castle responded by removing him from the Deputy Lieutenantship of County Monaghan, and from his position as Justice of the Peace, as well as reprimanding him for his 'language of studied insult to the Government of the Queen'. Much controversy ensued, and John Madden retired from public life to devote himself to travel and exploration, producing a geography book called *The Wilderness and Its Tenants.*

He also wrote *A History of the Madden family and their estates in Counties Leitrim, Monaghan and Fermanagh* in 1881 with the epigraph in Spanish: *Nacimos arreglando, vivimos arreglando, y por fin, moriremos sin haber arreglado nada.* (We were born putting things in order, we lived putting things in order, and in the end, we will die without having put anything in order.)

In 1886, he wrote a pamphlet 'A Few Remarks Upon The Irish Crisis': 'It is neither high rents nor oppressive landlords that have caused the Irish poverty and misery. It is the hopeless struggle of cottier tenants to maintain themselves and their families upon plots of land wholly inadequate for the purpose. These cottiers, in fact, constitute, in one word, what may be termed Volcanic Ireland, steeped as they are to the lips in ignorance and misery.' His great-great-grandson was now attending school with the descendants of these Volcanic Irelanders.

Johnny Madden, when he came back from Clones, showed me a commonplace book he himself kept with a quotation from an Indian chief his great-grandfather had met, which Johnny thought was appropriate for the position of the Protestant in Southern Ireland: 'We were born under the shadow of those trees; and our fathers' bones were buried beneath them. Should we say to the bones of our forefathers: "Arise and come with us into a foreign land?" ' I flicked through the book, finding another quotation which said: 'The essence of a free democracy is not that majorities should prevail, but rather that minorities should consent'. He pointed me to another one which came from a

Fianna Fail politician, Fianna Fail being the largest political party
in the Republic: 'You have to understand how Fianna Fail thinks.
The party works out which side of an issue will win electorally,
and that's the side it will always be on: the winning side.'

The storm had cleared by morning. Johnny seemed hesitant
when I went to settle accounts with him; he wasn't happy dealing
with bills and money. He offered to drive me to Clones. During
the hunger strike in 1981, he said, when things were tense in
Monaghan as well as in the North, he was worried that Hilton
Park would be burned by the locals; he was afraid to leave the
house in case it was set on fire. One of the workmen told him
there was no danger. The locals had agreed in the pub that the
Maddens had long given people work when there was no work
elsewhere. He was in Dublin with his father, still worried about
the house, as the hunger strikers began to die in Long Kesh. The
Gardaí kept a watch on the house, even though they confided in
him that they did not think the house was in danger.

'Ye bought your land,' a Garda said to Johnny Madden. He
meant that the Maddens had not come to Scothouse during a
Plantation or Confiscation. In 1732 they had bought the land.
People remembered.

8

The Walls of Derry

I went back to Derry by bus for the Apprentice Boys' Parade on the twelfth of August. When I had found a guesthouse and deposited my bags, I took a walk around the city, which was quiet, almost desolate at seven o'clock in the evening. Just as I was going into a pub for a drink, I met Eamonn McCann, who had been involved in the early civil-rights marches in Derry and had written *War And An Irish Town*, the best account of the early days of unrest in Derry in 1969 and 1970. We went to a few pubs around the centre of the city, which ranged from the dingy and downbeat to the disco bar.

Later, as we walked back to the McCanns' house in the Bogside, he stopped and stood on a piece of waste ground at the side of St Eugene's Cathedral and looked at the skyline of Derry. So much was missing now, so much bombed to bits, including the huge monument to General Walker who had led the Apprentice Boys in 1689. McCann wondered if it hadn't been a mistake blowing up the monument; perhaps, he mused, it would have been better to have taken Walker down and put up somebody else. He couldn't think who.

McCann pointed to a block of flats where the singer Dana, who won the Eurovision Song Contest in 1970 with a song called 'All Kinds Of Everything', used to live on the seventh floor. He was there when she came back to Derry after the contest, and the crowd went wild on the street beneath her balcony; they wanted her to come out and sing the song for them, the song which had won the Eurovision title not for the United Kingdom – of which the people of Derry were officially members – but for the Irish Republic, just a few miles over the border, which they wanted to be citizens of. When she made an appearance they cheered and roared and she sang for them:

Snowdrops and daffodils, butterflies and bees,
Sail boats and fishing nets, things of the seas,
Wishing wells, wedding bells, early morning dew,
All kinds of everything remind me of you.

They were delighted with her, one of their own, and when more people came along and joined the crowd, she sang the song again; those in the street felt that it was a great day for Derry and for Ireland. So proud of Dana, and Derry, did the crowd become and so enthusiastic generally, that a major riot began, which ended in the destruction of an entire street of warehouses, causing several million pounds' worth of damage.

*

Down off the Diamond in Derry the following morning, strong scaffolding and black canvas prevented anyone from peering into the Catholic Bogside, or hurling down stones at the people there from the walls. The British army and the RUC stood guard, preventing anyone from tearing down the scaffolding. Inside the Apprentice Boys' Hall was Peter Robinson, who had led his followers into the hated South in the reaches of the night, where they had frightened the people of the village of Clontibret in County Monaghan.

He had made the headlines, and now the photographers were waiting to snap Peter Robinson. Young men stood about with cans of beer in their hands looking at the photographers.

'Ulster will always fucking say no,' one of them said.

Robinson, when he came out, was young, mild and lean like a greyhound. He carried an umbrella, and wore a blue shirt, smiling wanly. He did not look like a hero; nor did he have that cold, frightening look which journalists worldwide had ascribed to him. He looked plain and ordinary, and seemed alert, quite smart, confident.

Everyone wanted to touch him, shake his hand, greet him. As he walked through Derry that morning he was met with great warmth. His minder made sure he kept moving, watching out all the time for potential assailants. The photographers followed him, their cameras clicking as the women greeted him, as the youths waved a Union Jack from the walls of Derry, and he waved back at them as he passed.

Apart from his minder, Robinson walked alone. The bridge across the Foyle was already full of marchers in their sashes and their bowler hats. The lines of marchers were facing towards Robinson as he walked across the bridge. He had timed this brilliantly. Everyone saw him, shouted at him, noticed him, the man of the moment, the deputy who had outshone his leader, Ian Paisley, in zeal.

Suddenly, we were in the Waterside. A great crowd had gathered around Robinson, and a smaller group had collected around Paisley. The streets were full of tension. There were no police anywhere. I started glancing nervously around. I wanted to get out of there. If I opened my mouth they would know I was from the South of Ireland. The Protestant loyalists, unlike their Catholic counterparts, had a deep suspicion of journalists.

Some of the young men seemed drunk already. They stood in groups, their expressions grim. I tried to move back towards the bridge, but there were too many people in the street, and I was afraid to push, afraid someone would notice the early stages of panic. I bought a pamphlet with the Union Jack on the front of it, but I still felt that I looked like an outsider. I edged in against the wall, and stood with my back to a shop window. I was sure someone would come at me from behind. There was no humour in this gathering, no sense of enjoyment, no feeling that these people were on an excursion or a day out.

I felt that if any violence broke out, if they started attacking anyone – me, for instance – it would be serious. I felt that anyone who drew their anger could be badly beaten. I saw a photographer I knew wandering around with a group of American photographers. He told me in whispers that one of them had been kicked on the way across the bridge. I whispered to him that I thought we should get out now. He seemed anxious in case anyone would notice how worried we looked: we were out of our depth.

We moved slowly back away from where Robinson and Paisley were still greeting their supporters, and edged our way towards the bridge. The march was beginning; the music of the accordions, the pipes and drums filled the air. We moved back towards the city centre, there to get a better and safer view of the march. I felt I was stupid to have followed Robinson for so long. I wasn't going to do that again.

As they came into the Diamond, the marchers, the Apprentice Boys, removed their hats as they passed the monument to those killed in the war. Shipquay Street was blocked by RUC jeeps. Police and army stood about; they were jeered by some of the groups who passed by, especially a black soldier at whom they shouted 'Nigger', 'Blackie' and 'Darkie'.

There were bands from all over the North. Pipe bands wearing kilts, pipe bands wearing purple dicky bows, pipe bands with two little boys in front throwing batons up in the air and catching them with immense skill. There were accordion bands, too, dressed in red, white and blue. Even young ones marching, the teenagers, had a severe look on their faces.

Each band had a banner dedicated to King William himself, who had saved Ulster from Popery, or General Walker who had led the resistance to the siege, or some other figure from the mythology of Unionism, with a slogan such as 'No Surrender' and the name of the band's place of origin. Some of them came from across the border.

Each band, too, had men carrying swords, one of whom I followed along for some time, enjoying the look of pleasure, importance and pomposity on his face. Others had men carrying huge ceremonial batons, or sticks. Coleraine had a man dressed up like a general. The Sons of Ulster, Carrickfergus had a skinhead out in front with a heavy stick in his hand; as he came around the corner he let out a yowl, and glared ahead as though daring anyone to deny him his right to do so. A few boys with National Front T-shirts stood about and watched the parade as well. A branch from Liverpool passed by. A man stuck out his tongue at the RUC.

Afterwards, I went down into the Bogside to see what our Catholic brethren had been doing while their compatriots had been celebrating their deliverance in 1689. On Shipquay Street the RUC drew their batons and went in pursuit of a few youths;

otherwise it was all calm. It was even quieter as I turned left, walked past a few RUC jeeps and made my way along towards the Bogside.

My mind was on something else. I was walking along without paying the slightest attention to what was around me. I was swiftly and suddenly brought down to earth by a Derry accent: 'Get out of the way.' Right in front of me were two blokes both wearing balaclava helmets over their faces, slits for their eyes, both moving forward cautiously towards the corner. It didn't take long for me to realize that what they had in their hands were petrol bombs. I ran across the street to a café which had begun to pull its shutters down.

They threw the petrol bombs and ran, removing the balaclavas, so that within a few seconds it was impossible to distinguish them from ordinary passers-by. As soon as the bombs exploded the RUC jeeps careered into the street and the café filled up with people running for cover. I could hear the sound of rubber bullets being fired.

When the noise died down, they pulled up the shutters of the café again and I moved towards Rossville Street. People had come out of the houses and the flats and were standing around. Six different television crews had placed themselves at strategic points on the waste ground all around. Photographers were everywhere. I watched some children putting on balaclava helmets and leading a group of photographers up a side alley. Most of the photographers were foreign. Someone pointed out to me a man who was standing among the crowd as a senior member of the IRA, who was watching over things.

A boy, who couldn't be more than ten years of age, moved out from the crowd and threw a stone at the RUC jeep. He ran back and emerged again with another stone. He didn't bother putting on a mask. A few RUC jeeps moved around the piece of waste ground, but did not come any closer. Further down the Bogside a few kids had lit a bonfire on the street. A youth was wandering around wearing a pink balaclava helmet. A helicopter flew overhead.

The photographers in the Bogside and the camera crews who had stayed in the Bogside had not done well that afternoon. Had they ventured across the river to the Waterside they would have witnessed a battle between the RUC and the more militant of the loyalist marchers. Such a battle would have been unthinkable before the Anglo-Irish Agreement.

A few photographers had snapped up that battle, and sat having dinner in an Indian restaurant. They were delighted with themselves. An American photographer and her French colleague were making a deal whereby she would give her photos to his agency and he would pay her. An Iranian photographer was trying to contact Paris and other faraway capitals from the coin box, and returned constantly to our table bemoaning the fact that he couldn't get through.

Later that night in the Catholic Bogside, a hijacked Ulsterbus blocked Rossville Street and groups of people stood around the flats. On the left one whole block of flats was in the process of being demolished by the authorities; everything had been cleared out except the outside walls, the floors and the walls between the flats. You could look up at this shell, and see the wallpaper, the few light fittings left, and the tiny, cramped spaces where whole families had been reared. The place resembled a giant empty book case towering over the journalists and photographers waiting for a riot to begin and the locals who were obligingly preparing to put on a show for them.

When the pubs were well shut, and everyone was assembled, a few blokes wearing masks went into the bus and covered it with petrol. We stood back and watched them douse the seats and the floor and then set the bus alight before running back into an alleyway. The bus began to burn, slowly at first, but then with increasing ferocity. As it burned, it was decided by whoever was controlling this event that more material was needed; a French journalist and a BBC journalist were forced to hand over their cars, which were driven up and down the road with enormous relish by a group of local teenagers before they were handed back, undamaged.

The burning bus revved for a while, as though a phantom driver had started the ignition. Then the fire died down. 'Now that it's gone out I'm cold,' said an American photographer. I was cold too, and decided that it was time to go home. I was going to Clones the following day to resume my walk along the border. I walked up the road to my lodgings. As I passed a group of new houses, a car pulled in and a number of middle-aged women got out. They looked at me.

'Would you like some apple pie?' one of them asked. 'Come on, have some, we'd hate it to go to waste.' In her hand was a covered-over dish of apple pie. She had no knife, or fork, or spoon, so she made me take it with my hands. Take more, take more, she insisted. The other women got out of the car, and someone came out of the house; they all stood around at three in the morning, the burnt-out bus just around the corner, and encouraged me to finish the pie, laughing and joking, delighted that they had found a hungry young man on his way home.

*

If any town in Ireland deserved a hero it was the border town of Clones where I went the next day. Signs of former prosperity were everywhere, I could see them as soon as I arrived from Derry: the old railway buildings, for example, the market house or the banks on the Diamond. The town was important as a place where rail lines crossed, a northern version of Limerick junction, an Irish version of Crewe. The northern railways were closed in 1959. Clones was also cut off from the North, its hinterland; the road was cut at Lackey Bridge on the border. It was a town which had gone to sleep. It was also a town in which three or four hundred copies of the Provos' newspaper *An Phoblacht* were sold every week.

I was in Clones on the night Barry McGuigan lost his title as World Featherweight Champion to a young Texan, Steve Cruz. I had come late at night, as the match was not scheduled until after one in the morning. The town was empty, the pubs seemed shut, a couple of Gardaí walked the streets. It struck me that Clones had become used to McGuigan fights. On the occasion of the victory over Pedroza which gave him the title, the place had gone crazy; drinking and carousing went on for days. The night of the second fight against Cabrera had been quieter. It was possible that McGuigan fever was petering out.

McGuigan was a local boy whose family had a shop in the

centre of the town. His father had been a singer who once represented Ireland in the Eurovision Song Contest. People were proud of McGuigan, and they expected him to win tonight. I knocked on the side door of The Paragon, which had a glimmer of light showing through the blinds, and I was let in. The television was down in the back room, where the writer Eugene McCabe was having a drink with his family. Eugene McCabe's house was a few miles down the road, just on the border; he was related to McGuigan by marriage. There wouldn't be much excitement tonight, he assured me. People were used to McGuigan winning, and the fight was on too late for a massive audience in the pubs of Clones, he said.

We sat around waiting for the fight to begin. There were some drinkers in the front bar; the back bar was half empty. It was the middle of the day in Las Vegas where the fight was to take place, and McGuigan's only problem would be the heat. We paid scant attention to the preliminaries.

It was after one o'clock now, and people were tired. The bar was still serving. Just after the film of McGuigan weighing in, I noticed that there was a crowd in the bar, all carefully placed so they could see the television. In a few minutes the place had filled up. Eugene McCabe's sister-in-law hated boxing, and would never watch it, she said, but because of McGuigan, she had to see it. I could see her becoming nervous as the fight began.

Everyone became tense. Only between rounds would people sip their drinks or talk to each other, or move places. People in the bar stayed still when the fight was on, their faces intent, watching the screen, shouting encouragement when McGuigan seemed close to hitting Cruz. McGuigan seemed in no danger during the first few rounds, but the fight was still exciting, and the excitement could be felt throughout the bar, as though the match were going on right in front of us, as though McGuigan could hear the cries of support.

Rounds four and five were good for McGuigan, who forced Cruz up against the ropes and punched at his body. Eugene's sister-in-law covered her face with her hands each time either boxer was punched. The crowd in the bar just wanted McGuigan to win. The support was becoming louder and more aggressive. 'Hit him, Barry, hit him.'

Towards the end of round six, people began to realize that something funny was going on. A left hook to the jaw knocked McGuigan across the ring; Cruz kept working away at McGuigan's head. But Barry had been in trouble before, and he was clearly winning. The crowd at Las Vegas could be heard singing 'Here We Go, Here We Go, Here We Go'. But the next round was even worse for McGuigan, with Cruz hammering away at his head. People in the bar were now standing up on the seats, screaming at McGuigan, as though he was close by, as though he could hear them.

The next two rounds were better; some of the tension eased, and it seemed just a matter of time before McGuigan would be declared the winner. He needed staying power, that was all, because it looked as though the match was going to last the full fifteen rounds.

In the middle of round ten, Cruz knocked McGuigan to the ground. It seemed impossible, he was having trouble getting up. There were cries and screams in the bar. People had their hands over their mouths, as though they had witnessed some appalling accident. 'Come on, Barry,' someone shouted. 'Come on, come on, come on.' Eugene's sister-in-law had her head in her hands. I could hear the people breathing around me as we waited for the next round to begin.

During the next two rounds it seemed as though the people in the pub were themselves being beaten and punched in the head until they fell against the ropes. Every time McGuigan was hit someone would let out a scream. 'Barry, Barry,' they kept calling him, sometimes in whispers. When they said 'Come on, Barry' now there was a new tone, as though he had paid no attention to them before; they were urging him, hectoring him, imploring him. 'Come on, Barry.' After round twelve there was silence: no one had anything to say. He was losing. He was going to have to do something.

McGuigan was brilliant in round thirteen. The fear which he had displayed for the first time, the timid look in his eye, had gone now. He was on the attack. He hurt Cruz and went after him with more blows. He was going to do it, he was going to win; this was what he needed to do; he was winning. The bar was jubilant. All he had to do was keep out of trouble for the next two rounds, and he would win on points.

In the next round he was playing for time, keeping the show on the road. One more round and he would win on points. I was sure about that. But the final round was a disaster. No one could believe what was happening. The men and women in the bar kept shrieking at the television. There was consternation when he went down. He looked groggy and dazed. That look of defeat, which I had seen in round ten, came back into his face. Everyone saw it, recognized it instantly. This had never happened before: he was going to lose. People could barely look up as he was knocked down a second time. There was an intensity in the way they called to him, called out his name.

Then there was a delay as the judges came to their conclusion. People around me started discussing the possibility of McGuigan winning on points. I said that I didn't think he was going to win. 'Don't say that,' someone turned to me. 'Don't say that.' But it was too late. The judges declared Cruz the new World Featherweight Champion.

As soon as this happened, everyone got ready to leave. Nobody wanted to have another drink, nobody spoke. The television began to show the last round again, to be met with howls from the pub to turn it off, turn it off. Nobody wanted to watch it again, everybody wanted to get home, away from it. 'This is the worst thing which has happened in this town since they closed the railway in 1959,' Eugene's nephew said to me as he passed by.

*

I walked out of Clones the next day, northwards in the direction of Lackey Bridge. It was a warm day, with a hazy sunlight. County council workers trimming the ditches with scythes were able to show me where the North began and continued along a stretch of the road and stopped again to make way for the South. They had heard of helicopters landing on this little patch, but didn't think it happened much. A mile beyond was Eugene McCabe's house, Dromard, taking its name from *drom*, meaning ridge and *ard* meaning high. The house was on a small hill with beech trees around it; most of the land was in the South, but one corner was in the North.

Eugene was a farmer as well as a writer. He kept a herd of Jersey cows, and he was trying to cut a field of silage before more rain came and made the fields unuseable once more. The house was beautiful, although its comforts were modest and unobtrusive. It was old, a big new picture window in the dining room was the only modern element; the decor was faded, the colours muted without being drab.

From the long window on the stairway, you could look north and see the British army post. Eugene's wife Margôt wondered if they noticed every time someone went up and down the stairs. Although the army had a checkpoint in the North, just beyond the bridge, the road was still closed at Lackey Bridge, the usual concrete and spikes blocking the way. It was first spiked in 1957, re-opened in the early 1960s, and blocked again in 1980.

I went down to look at the bridge with Margôt while Eugene was about his farming business. All the farms on the other side of the small river were owned by Protestants. She pointed out the various houses. At one time, there had been a great deal of contact between the two sides, but now there was none. Over to the left there was a point at which cars could cross the stream, but this had now been blocked up. Beside it stood an abandoned house, which had once been owned by a woman who used to work in Dromard for Margôt.

To the right of Lackey Bridge there was another road which had, at one time, led into a farm in the North, but this was now blocked as well, and the farmer had no exit in the South any more. It was sad, Margôt said, having neighbours you didn't meet any more. They had only discovered that one of their nearest neighbours' sons had got married several years after the event. She remembered a day in the summer, when her children were young, going across with them to a small shop run by a Protestant woman on the other side of the border. There were Protestant children there as well, and they were all too young to go to school and so too young to realize, in their separate Catholic and Protestant classrooms, that there were deep divisions between them. So that day they could play together, but soon they would go their different ways. It was strange watching them, knowing that.

Eugene and Margôt had made their own contribution to the possibility that this sectarianism would someday end, by sending their eldest son to a multi-denominational school. It now seemed a small gesture compared with what had happened over fifteen years along the Monaghan–Fermanagh border. Some called it genocide, believing that Protestants were being picked off because they were only sons, and a farm might then fall into Catholic hands. Everyone knew that the IRA had an information network which was effective and local, which could trace the movement of people they wanted to kill. Protestants had good reason to suspect their Catholic neighbours.

They felt under siege. In May 1981, one of them told the *Irish Times*: 'They want us off the land, out of business, they want us gone. We're the planters. That's the way we feel. That's the way we're made to feel. We're like the Rhodesians, we're like the Israelis. But we've been here for hundreds of years. We're not going to be intimidated. We're going to fight. There are plenty of deserted Protestant farms down in Fermanagh. Too many. It's not going to happen here.'

But there had been no fight, just more killings on isolated holdings year after year. The IRA justified this war of attrition by saying that UDR and RUC members were legitimate targets, members of a sectarian native security force backing up the British occupation. For the Protestants, however, the UDR men and RUC men were neighbours, often farmers, members of the same church, the same community. For them, it looked like genocide, organized, aided and abetted by the very people they passed on the road every day, who lived in the adjoining farms, but who went to worship in a Catholic chapel.

Eugene had written about this in two books, published in the 1970s, *Victims* and *Heritage*. He got the idea for *Heritage* from the woman who had lived in the abandoned house near Lackey Bridge, who helped clean at Dromard. She also worked across the border for the Johnstons. One day she mentioned casually that there was friction in the Johnstons' house, because the son

Ernest had joined the UDR. It stayed in Eugene's mind: the house, the cleaning woman, the family and the son in the UDR, the landscape.

The story opens with a hawk sweeping in to kill a pigeon in the farmyard. Eric O'Neill, a Protestant UDR man, watches it move away.

He followed its flight towards Shannock and Carn Rock, a dim, hidden country, crooked scrub ditches of whin and thorns stunted in sour putty land; bare spade-ribbed fields, rusted tin-roofed cabins, housing a stonyfaced people living from rangy cattle and Welfare handouts. From their gaunt lands they looked down on the green border country below, watching, waiting. To them a hundred years was yesterday, two hundred the day before.

'A rotten race,' George said, 'good for nothing but malice and murder; the like of Hitler would put them through a burnhouse and spread them on their sour bogs and he'd be right, it's all they're fit for.'

The lane sloped steeply to the county road. He walked by the orchard and beech copse planted by his grandfather in 1921 to block off the view of the Fenian South. He could see through the grey lichened trunks the slate coloured river winding through thick rushy bottoms past Inver Hall and Church towards Lough Erne. A week ago he had watched a gun fight between British soldiers and gunmen across the river in the Republic. He saw one human hit and dragged away by two others. His mouth was dry for hours after. Every other day these last few years their windows rattled from explosions in nearby towns and villages. Now since he had joined the UDR the thing had got ugly. Three men he knew were dead, two UDR, one Catholic policeman. Tonight when he put on his uniform his mother would be near tears. Every day when they talked about land, neighbours or cattle prices, they were thinking something else. He was a big target. He could be got handy. Death spitting from a gap or a bog, a sharp bend in the road, a cattle mart or shop counter, a body trapped between town-lands, or blown asunder on the

tractor drawing turf from Doon forest, where it seemed dark
now in July.

'It's a jungle from here to the rock,' a neighbour told him,
'they don't need phones, radios or helicopters; sneeze at the
back of a ditch, they know who it was and why he was there,
they know every move, we don't stand a chance.'

It is clear from the beginning how the story will end. Eric will
be killed, it is there in the first sentence.

Margôt and Eugene heard shooting one night as they were
going to bed; there was often shooting. It was the end of September 1980; *Heritage* had been published two years earlier. It was
only when they were driving to Dublin in the morning that they
discovered what had happened. Ernest Johnston, their neighbour
from the other side of the border, had been shot dead during the
night. His name was given on the radio, he was in the UDR.
They listened in the car, appalled. Even now six years later they
seemed shocked by it. The character in *Heritage* had been shot
dead, now the original had been shot as well.

9

The Killing Fields

For days on end the sky was grey. The roads were narrow. The land was soggy. For days on end I walked through a world haunted by two men. Everywhere I turned I heard about them. I learned certain facts about them, enough to compare and contrast them, as though the story was neat and tidy and could be pinned down.

One was a Catholic, the other a Protestant; one lived just south of the border, the other just north of the border, both died violently of bullet wounds in the same year, 1986, within a few miles of each other, one in April, one in July. Both had large funerals. It is possible that the man who died in July had been present as the first one died; it is even possible that the man who died in July was killed in reprisal for the first death; it is also possible that neither of these things is true; but it must be said that some people believed them.

Seamus McElwain, John McVitty.

When I left Eugene's house, I crossed Lackey Bridge on foot, and walked past the British army post. The first lane on the left led to McVitty's. John McVitty was shot dead by the IRA on 8 July, 1986. His farm was right on the border. The IRA had escaped across the fields and over Lackey Bridge into the South after the shooting. McVitty was an RUC man and a farmer. He was working in a field with his twelve-year-old son when they got him.

His sister, a local schoolteacher, and her husband lived in the next house on the left. Her sister-in-law, in turn, and her family lived on the right hand side, and beyond them Ernest Johnston's parents in a small house; Ernest Johnston's widow lived in a bungalow on the left-hand side.

Further up the road there were a large number of cars parked on the side of the road, something was on, an auction, a cattle

sale, and a few men stood at the side of the road watching me
suspiciously as I came close. They didn't return any greeting.
There was a 'Join the Ulster Clubs' sign further along before the
Catholic church, described in *Heritage* as 'a plain stucco barn-like
building, with a separate belfry, a white Madonna in a cave
between the church and the curate's bungalow'.

The curate was Father McCabe, the first civilian to see Seamus
McElwain dead. McElwain was shot dead by the SAS on 14 April,
1986. McElwain came from Scotstown in North Monaghan, and
had been officer in command of the County Fermanagh division
of the IRA before he was captured near Roslea by the RUC in
1981. He was later sentenced to a recommended thirty years
in prison. He stood in the Irish general election in February
1982, receiving four thousand votes as an H-Block candidate. He
escaped from the Maze in 1984 and continued to operate in the
South Fermanagh area until his death. There were over four
thousand people at his funeral.

This is how the local newspaper the *Northern Standard* reported
his death:

> In the neat two storeyed farmhouse among the hills of
> Knockatallon, lay the bullet-riddled body of a darkly hand-
> some young man in his coffin. The turbulent young life of
> Seamus McElwain had been brutally ended in a field only a few
> miles from his home.
>
> Now he was being waked as a soldier of Oglaigh na
> hEireann [the IRA] the army of his father's political creed
> in his farmer's house. It was a 'lying in state', with two stat-
> uesque figures dressed in the style of combat uniform with
> muffled face that has become identified with the IRA . . . He
> [McElwain] and a comrade, Sean Lynch, a young man from
> the Roslea area, were crossing a field about half a mile from
> Roslea village armed with two rifles when what is alleged to
> have been an SAS unit opened up on them from hiding. It
> is believed that the two young men were going to man a
> mine they had laid in a culvert on the Roslea-Donagh road
> some days before. It is thought that the British forces had
> detected the presence of the mine and staked it out.
>
> At break of day, about five a.m., on Saturday morning

last, the two IRA men were making their way towards the
terminal of the command wire. It is clear that the troops in
ambush opened fire on them without warning or call for
surrender.

The newspaper went on to quote Sean Lynch, who said that
there was no challenge or warning. 'He was hit in the stomach
and hand but jumped down into the field. He heard McElwain
falling down the ditch . . . He managed to struggle on about a
hundred yards before rolling into a drain and covering himself with
muck, leaves and branches . . . He could hear them interrogating
McElwain, shouting "Who was with you?" This went on for
some time, and then he heard three shots.'

The curate wasn't in when I called. I didn't wait, but tele-
phoned him later and asked when he had first heard of McElwain's
death. He was contacted by phone that morning, he said. He
thought it was just before eight. He was told that someone was
dead, the army would tell him more when he drove to the main
road. They gave no names or details. They wouldn't let him drive
along the main road into Roslea, so he made his way there along
the side roads and then out again to where the body was. He had
to wear wellingtons to cross the fields. What struck him as strange
was that he knew no one, all the army and RUC people were
strangers in the area. When they were just five feet from the body
he was told the name: Seamus McElwain. He knew him, as he
had been curate in Scotstown and knew the family. Even though
the body was lying face down, he would have recognized the
dead man. He was told that he could not move the body so he
found it difficult to give the last rites. He had to put his hand in
under the face to administer the oil, as the others watched.

*

Beyond Father McCabe's house, up a hill to the left, was the
Protestant church at Aghadrumsee. John McVitty was buried
there. I had been here before, at his funeral one grey day in the
summer. The small plain church was built on top of a drumlin
opposite the Orange Hall. It was the Protestant church in Eugene
McCabe's *Heritage*: 'a small Romanesque block all spikes and

parapets with one sharp spire to the front in two acres of burial ground'. I stood at the bottom of the hill, and watched the hearse approaching down a side road, where some of McVitty's former colleagues in the RUC waited to carry the coffin up to the church. Local people, neighbours of the McVittys, some politicians and RUC chiefs waited. There was a Union Jack on the coffin, as well as the dead policeman's cap.

It began to rain softly. Everything was modest and low key. The RUC men tried to carry the coffin as quietly as they could. The single tolls of the church bells were muted. The road was narrow, overhung by sycamore trees. It could have been a quiet country funeral anywhere in Ireland. The dead man's twelve-year-old son was in the back of the car which drove slowly up the hill after the coffin.

The church was full, so people stood among the headstones in the graveyard, or outside the gates where loudspeakers had been placed. The family, widow, sisters, daughters, one son, followed the coffin up the centre aisle of the church where they were met by the local bishop and clergyman. An 'Order of Service' had been printed with the date and the dead man's name as well as the readings, the hymns and the prayers.

'Fret not thyself because of the ungodly: neither be thou envious against the evil doers . . . For they shall soon be cut down like the grass: and be withered even as the green herb . . . The ungodly watcheth the righteous: and seeketh occasion to slay him . . .' The bishop read from the thirty-seventh psalm and from Paul's First Letter to the Corinthians.

'He [John McVitty] had,' he said in his sermon, 'embodied much of what it is to be a Church of Ireland member in these difficult times in the border counties of Northern Ireland, ready to put his life on the line, hard working and courageous, trying to serve the community in almost impossible circumstances.'

There was silence in the church and from the porch where I stood I could see the faces in the graveyard, listening to every word as though it might explain why another RUC man had been killed in their area, and why the killers had escaped so easily. The bishop went on to warn them not to cease cooperation with the police because of the Anglo-Irish Agreement; this would, he said, bring about anarchy.

When they had sung 'The Lord is My Shepherd', they were addressed by the local clergyman, the Reverend Kille. He described how the sound of a helicopter was not unusual around Roslea, but he knew the other evening as the helicopter came over just as himself and his wife were sitting down to tea that there was something wrong. A few moments later they received a phone call from a distressed parishioner to tell them that tragedy had struck once more, and they went to the scene of ravage and destruction which they had seen too often before. His voice was dramatic, his delivery highly charged with emotion. His audience was listening carefully as he told them to turn to Jesus for comfort. The rain had stopped outside.

He went on to speak of how 'the invisible hosts of good and evil are joined in battle'. He mentioned Seamus McElwain's funeral in Scotstown just a few months before, and wondered how such a man could have been given all the honours of his church, with three priests in attendance, and 'made to look like the greatest of heroes and the greatest of saints'. 'Civil obedience,' he said, 'and the gospel are linked together like knife and fork, husband and wife.'

He started to name the names of those who had been killed in Fermanagh since the Troubles started. He paused between each name in his litany; he went down through them, some of them well known atrocities, keenly remembered, others old headlines, long forgotten, names on a headstone somewhere. Sometimes he gave just the name, and sometimes he mentioned if they belonged to the security forces, sometimes he mentioned their profession or business. His voice became more emotional as his long list went on. There were over seventy names to be read out, Protestant names mostly, and each person in the congregation would have known at least one of them. There was a note of warning implied in what he was saying: that those listening were also perhaps suitable candidates for this list.

Towards the back of the graveyard a number of RUC men with rifles began to appear as the clergyman ended his list by saying that only one man had ever been convicted of any of these seventy-odd killings and he was 'allowed to escape from the Maze'. The man he had in mind was Seamus McElwain.

There was anger now in his voice. 'We live in no-go land,' he said. 'We feel that something ought to be done for us so that the past will not be repeating itself over and over again.' The heads in the graveyard were bowed now, people seemed anxious to avoid each others' eyes. 'John was a brave man,' he continued, telling of how he could have gone to the police in Canada, but had stayed instead to serve his country. The congregation sang 'Abide With Me', and the coffin was carried from the church to the grave. Near John McVitty's grave were two other graves of UDR men, the words 'murdered by the IRA' were etched in parentheses on their gravestones after their names.

*

Now, a couple of months later, I came to a crossroads, with a small shop in a temporary building, the permanent one having been bombed. On the opposite side of the road was an old barn bearing a 'Join the Ulster Clubs' sign, and the letters UFF, standing for Ulster Freedom Fighters, a Protestant paramilitary group. I took the right turn towards Roslea. It was a fine day, and I was able to walk for a while in my shirtsleeves without a pullover. I was watching for a bungalow on the right; I had been told that there was a teacher there who knew the area.

I knocked on a few doors until I found the right house. The teacher was a man in his thirties, who worked in the local national school. He was a Catholic. Seamus McElwain had been killed not far from here. The army had been jubilant about getting McElwain, he said. They had stopped his car and said to him: 'We got McElwain last Saturday, we'll get the rest of you yet.' He had been very upset by this.

There was no contact now between Protestant schoolchildren and their Catholic counterparts, he said, even though there were large sums of money available for interdenominational activity. 'We'd be willing,' he said, 'but they don't want to know.' The principal of the local Protestant school was a sister of John McVitty's, he said.

Clones was just four miles away, but since Lackey Bridge was closed it was now eleven miles in a car, and local people didn't go there any more. He warned me about walking around the area at night, particularly the road to Fivemiletown, where I would be likely to meet the UDR patrols, all local Protestants. 'There's no hope until they're disbanded,' he said.

He used to work as a presiding officer during elections, but things had become too bitter, he said, and so he stopped. He was present at a killing in 1979 in the school where he taught. He had come to work one morning and walked into the school kitchen, to find the caretaker and the kitchen staff sitting at a table. He had asked what was going on, but was met with silence. Then he saw a hooded man beside the door who asked him who he was. Another hooded man appeared in the room as well.

It was clear that they were waiting to kill someone, but the staff had no idea who. Names went through all their minds; they didn't even know which side the hooded men were on – they might have come to shoot a teacher with Republican sympathies.

He asked them to let him go and get the children out of the way. 'None of the children will be harmed,' they said, and told him to shut up. Soon the staff discovered that the two hooded men were waiting for Herbie, who came on certain days in a delivery van. He was a part-time UDR man. They must have had inside information of what days and at what time he came. They had arrived early that morning and surprised the caretaker, taking the keys of his car. Later, they would use the car to escape, and it would never be found again.

They waited in the school for the sound of a van to approach, knowing that if Herbie was there, as he always was, then he was going to be killed. The two hooded men told them to lie down on the floor, and not to raise the alarm for ten minutes. Then the van came. The staff heard the sharp, piercing sound of the gunfire. Herbie hadn't got a chance. They pumped twenty-one bullets into him, having got up close to him. Some of the children would have seen it. Their teacher sat opposite me in his living room, and asked me to imagine the effect it had on them. There was, he said, screaming and hysterics. The killers escaped over the border.

I left him and walked on towards Roslea. I was walking faster now as the afternoon faded. I had an appointment with the clergyman who had delivered the sermon at John McVitty's funeral. His house, he had told me, was a short distance from Roslea on the right, but when I enquired about its whereabouts from two young lads I met on the road, they couldn't believe their ears. Was I really looking for the Reverend Kille, they asked? Not many people went to his house, they told me, and pointed me towards it on the right-hand side.

He was working at a word processor in the front room of his house when he saw me coming, and stood up to let me in. On the wall of his office was a board with the photographs of several RUC men pinned on to it, as well as the scene of several bombings. They were the sort of photos you saw in the newspaper after a bombing or a shooting. I recognized one of the RUC men as McVitty.

Reverend Kille was minister, he told me, to three parishes, two of which were just over the border in the South. He began to list local people who had been killed by the IRA. He was amazed, he said, at the resilience of individuals who had been bereaved. 'The thing hurts too much, people would put up with this loss if they felt it was going to bring peace any nearer. People aren't frightened out of their inheritance easily.'

In 1981, when Bobby Sands, then on hunger strike in Long Kesh, ran for election and won thirty thousand votes, tensions were high in Fermanagh, he said; it caused people to say: 'We always thought it, now we've got the proof.' In voting for Sands, their Catholic neighbours were saying: 'We're for the IRA, we're for war.'

The Catholic Church, he said, speaks with two voices. One of them was heard at McElwain's funeral, the same voice at another IRA funeral where the priest said: 'The dead IRA man was a good boy and God will reward him,' the same voice when Pope Benedict the Fifteenth, according to a document which Reverend Kille showed me, gave his blessing to the rebels in 1916. The other voice was used for the condemnation of IRA activities by the same church leaders.

'I think it is basically a moral question. People should put the sanctity of life before everything else. Protestant paramilitaries have not had the same running as the Republicans, because by and large they are not accepted by the churches. The whole Protestant ethic is against any form of disloyalty to the governing process. The Protestant ethic is "Fear God and Honour the King". Look at the Protestants in the South, they have knuckled under.

'I don't know what Catholic grievances are. In Fermanagh we are the second-class citizens. I could name you a dozen firms in Fermanagh where there's not a Protestant employed.'

I told him that most of the good land in the border areas was in Protestant hands. He would not accept this. The Catholic land was bad only because they hadn't worked it properly; no land should be bad in this day and age, he said. 'The welfare state supplies everything they need,' he said.

Mixed marriages, he said, caused heartache. The two churches' ethics were so different. Rome was authoritarian, gave its flock no opportunity of choice. The Protestant ethic was harder because it said: 'This is your duty. You ought to do it.' But it didn't make you do it. There had been no marriages between Protestants and Catholics in his parish north of the border since 1974.

My time was up; he was busy, his word processor beckoned. It was difficult to argue with him; he was sure of himself. But I was sure that he was wrong when he said at John McVitty's funeral that only one IRA man was convicted of any of the seventy-odd killings in Fermanagh. But he insisted that he was right, and there was no point in producing names and dates for him of other IRA men who were serving sentences for some of these killings. He went back to his work, and I went back to the road. He gave me a map of the places where all the killings had taken place over fifteen years.

*

The first sign that Roslea remained steadfast in its opposition to the Crown, and all the Crown stood for, came in the first pub I went into. I asked for change to make a phone call, and was handed an Irish fifty-pence coin, worth less than its British counterpart, and told to give it back if I didn't get through.

I went to see a local Sinn Fein activist who lived in a council

estate in the town. The UDR didn't come to Roslea, he said,
they would be afraid. The place still had scars going back a long
way. The town had been burned in 1920 during the War of
Independence by the Black and Tans, a special division of the
British army as infamous in Ireland as Cromwell, as a reprisal for
an IRA shooting. Exactly a month later the IRA burned out
sixteen Protestant houses in the area and killed two members of
the B-Specials, the forerunners of the UDR. 'There had always
been,' he said, 'a history of resistance.'

Was shooting local men who were members of the RUC and
the UDR part of this resistance? 'When people are members of the
security forces, or rather the forces of occupation, they put their
necks at risk,' he said. The fire was lighting in the front room of
his council house. His wife brought in tea, brown bread and
biscuits. Did he know Seamus McElwain, I asked him?

Yes, he did. He smiled. 'He was likeable, dedicated, he believed
there was a job to be done,' he said. He went on to talk about
McElwain's death.

He said that there was a gap of twenty minutes, according to
local people who had heard gunfire, between the first shots and
the last. The other man who was with McElwain only managed
to survive by hiding after he was hit in the first burst of gunfire
from the SAS. If they had found him they would have killed him
in cold blood, my informant said. This, he claimed, was what
they did to McElwain. The RUC came and shot him while the
SAS held him. There were people, he said, who believed that
John McVitty, shot recently over at Lackey Bridge, whose funeral
I had been to, was the man who had encouraged them to shoot
McElwain dead, but he had no more evidence than what he had
heard people say.

The last year of McElwain's life would have been difficult, he
said. The Gardaí in the South were looking for him, as much as
the RUC in the North. He would have had no social life, no
money. 'A guerrilla is a fish that swims in the sea,' he said. The
sea was the small holdings of North Monaghan which would have
taken McElwain in, looked after him, offered him shelter. Seamus
McElwain may have killed a number of people, he said, but he
would never have done what the security forces did to him:

letting him bleed painfully to death in a ditch before finishing him off. 'You continually get the impression when you're discussing him that you're leaving something out,' he said. 'Sheamie was special, he is not a person whom words could describe.'

There was no hotel or guest house in Roslea and it was getting dark. It was a choice between the narrow, mountainous road to Fivemiletown, or the main road to Monaghan. I stood out on the main road to Monaghan and began hitching a lift. Within a few minutes, a big, powerful car pulled up, with a girl in her early twenties in the driver's seat, alone in the car. She asked me where I was going. I told her I was going to Monaghan. As I put on my safety belt, she said she was going there too. Twenty minutes later, she dropped me in the main square.

It was raining the next morning. Wet, gnawing rain like toothache. 'August rots all,' said a character in one of Eugene McCabe's stories. I could imagine the fields rotting all around me as August came to an end, full of muck and mire.

I decided to walk in the direction of Scotstown, into the big lump which County Monaghan cuts into the North. The desolation which is North Monaghan had not yet started and, despite the weather, some of the land looked good. There were old trees around the houses. I passed by an enormous acreage of glasshouses, most of them shattered and broken down, on the road into Bellanode.

Bellanode itself was remarkably well kept, with a landscaped garden by the bridge, a warning to visitors about litter, flowers in pots on the windowledges, garden seats on the footpaths, a beautiful old Protestant church with a plaque to the Wood Wright family, a well-tended graveyard; the legacy of Monaghan's Protestant heritage.

Scotstown, a few miles further north, was completely different. The first thing I saw when I arrived was an open-air garage, surrounded by quietly rusting cars. The place was sleepy and unkempt. I went into the first pub I came to. There was dead silence, the men at the bar stared over, said nothing, looked into their drinks. No one made any secret of the fact that I wasn't welcome. A man began to talk loudly about strangers wanting to know his business, and how no one had the right to tell anybody

anything about him other than his name. He didn't want anyone
even to say where he lived, he said. I finished my drink and left.

The windows of the Garda station, to the right, were covered
in wire, and it looked as though you had to speak into an intercom
before admission could be gained to the premises. I walked back
down to the main street again, and noticed a man watching me
from the door of a public house. He went inside as I approached.
The pub was Moyna's.

The Moyna twins, Tommy and Mackey, were county foot-
ballers for Monaghan in the 1950s. Mackey lived in Dublin; some
time previously bugging equipment had been discovered in his
house, which had caused a huge fuss in Dublin in the press and
the Dáil. Charlie Haughey, then leader of the opposition, insisted,
as did many others, that the bugging equipment had been placed
there by the Gardaí. Opinion was divided as to the motive: one
camp believed that it was because the SDLP Deputy Leader,
Seamus Mallon, stayed in the house when he was in Dublin;
another that the reason the house was bugged was that Mackey
Moyna's nephew Donal, from Scotstown, also stayed in the house,
and he was facing serious explosives charges, of which he was
later acquitted.

I went into the pub and sat up at the bar. The owner,
whom I took to be Tommy Moyna, was looking at a photograph
of a football team from the 1950s with a younger man and a lorry
driver who was delivering supplies of drink to the pub. They
were going through each face, each name, Tommy was well
informed on where each man was now, who was alive, who was
dead, who was in England, who was in America, who still lived
nearby, who had moved to Dublin. So intense was this inspection
of the photograph that it took them a while to notice me.

As soon as he looked up, Mr Moyna asked me my name and
my reason for being in North Monaghan. He knew who I was;
we had a mutual acquaintance in Dublin, who had written the
story of what became known as 'The Moyna Bugging Scandal'
with great gusto. He invited me to stay and have my tea when I
had finished my drink. I ordered a glass of lemonade.

I told him I had walked from Monaghan and passed through
Bellanode. He knew Bellanode. There had been big changes

there, he said. In 1945, a Union Jack had been raised over the Protestant church in neutral Ireland when the Second World War ended. At that time 95 per cent of the population of Bellanode was Protestant. In fact, he could think of only two Catholic families who were there at that time. Now three-quarters of the people there were Catholics; the Protestant school was turned into a bungalow, and the old Royal Irish Constabulary barracks was a dwelling house. Where had the Protestants gone? I asked him. 'Into the North, England, Canada, South Africa,' he said.

The name of the parish was Urbleshanny rather than Scotstown, *eirbeall* meaning 'tail' and *sionnach* meaning 'fox'. Mr Moyna had no idea why a village should be called Fox's Tail. The local post office, however, had its own view on the nomenclature of the place. It had *Baile an Scotaigh* proudly written over its doorway, *baile* meaning 'town', *an* meaning 'the', or 'of the', *Scotaigh* meaning nothing at all, being the English word 'Scot' placed in the Irish genitive case (the Irish for Scotland was *Albán*). So the name over the post office was a load of old nonsense, a piece of mis-translation. Mr Moyna, who was a nationalist and a member of Charlie Haughey's Fianna Fail Party, and myself both wondered about this piece of post-colonial confusion.

Scotstown was different from Bellanode, he said. It was a Catholic village with a strong Republican tradition, which was why the Garda station had wire over the windows. The hiring fairs had gone on here too until the early 1940s. Most of the Catholic holdings were too small to keep a family, so the children would be sent to work on the bigger Protestant farms which lay on the better land in the county. The biggest event in recent years, he said, was the funeral of Seamus McElwain, which took place in Scotstown, less than a hundred yards away. It was a big funeral. His family were local; he was popular.

There was a man at the bar who knew the family, as did Mr Moyna, and this man offered to drive me out to see them. Seamus's parents lived in Knockatallon, he said. It wasn't too far away. I said I didn't know if I wanted to talk to them.

The news came on with reports of a number of Unionists on a visit to a summer school which commemorated the navvy poet Patrick McGill in Donegal.

'A good mortar bomb wouldn't do them boys any harm,' the man at the bar said to me. I went into the Moyna's kitchen for a big fry-up and loads of hot tea. When I went back out the man was still at the bar.

'Come on, I'll take you,' he said.

'Okay,' I replied.

He drove along the narrow road, denouncing the Anglo-Irish Agreement.

'The only thing it has done for us is to cause the death of one of our volunteers,' he said. He was referring to McElwain.

Every single house in the area would have given shelter to McElwain during his time on the run, he said. Even people who didn't support him directly wouldn't have turned him away if he needed help.

The land we drove through was mainly bogland, which the summer rain had still not sunk through. The roads were narrow and straight. He drove me to a few places where the border bridges had been blown up by the British. At one point the road on the northern side had disappeared completely; the bog had folded over it, and it would never appear again, because it would never be needed again. The whole place was desolate now, depopulated, lonely; there wasn't much need for these small roads.

I dreaded arriving at the McElwain's house, having to ask them about their dead son, having to intrude into their grief. My driver said it would be okay; they were nice people, I musn't worry.

We drove down an extremely narrow road until we arrived at a small house. This was the McElwain's. The father wasn't in, but the mother was there milking the cows. She told us to go in, sit down, she would join us when she had finished.

There were several children in the house, who kept wandering in and out as we talked, sitting down, getting up, listening to the talk, leaving the room, coming back in. The mother sent one of them into the kitchen to make tea and sandwiches for us. She was a woman in her late forties perhaps, with a strong face.

What did I want to know about Seamus? she asked. She looked at me directly. What sort of person was he? I asked. It was a feeble question, but she took it seriously. He was kind, she said, he was a good son. He was popular; the attendance at his funeral had made that clear. He was prepared to die for his beliefs. He was a great Irish speaker, the driver interrupted. It was said about him that he knew more Irish than the teacher at school. He also knew the country, which was important during the escape from the Maze in 1984. He was instrumental, the driver said, in leading the group of escapees across difficult terrain.

I asked the mother how she had heard the news of his death. I could feel the tension rising in the room. It was the morning she said. She heard on the eight o'clock news that two IRA men had been intercepted while on an operation; one had been shot dead, the other injured. The Gardaí must have known then, she said, and the driver pointed out that the Gardaí must have given information to the British which caused Seamus and his colleague to be discovered.

She continued talking. Her account was precise and careful, as though the whole story was stored carefully in her memory, each detail, each thought. The Gardaí didn't come or telephone. She waited. There was a radio station Seamus always had faith in; he liked the news bulletins, and that was the station the dial was at. She listened at half past eight, at nine, at half past nine.

'And did you think your son had been shot?' I asked her.

'I thought nothing else,' she said. It rang out in the room like an appeal, louder and more intense than the rest of her story. She said it slowly, as though it caused her physical pain, each syllable given the same hard emphasis. The room was quiet. One of the children came in and started listening to her, another stood at the door of the kitchen and watched her as she told how she heard it on the ten o'clock news. It was him. He had been shot dead. It was only later when she and her husband went to see his companion in hospital that he told them that Seamus had been shot first in the legs and then left there, and was later shot in the stomach and then in the heart, how he was beaten and insulted during this period.

She heard nothing from the Gardaí until later that night, when they rang to say that if the family wished to have a quiet funeral rather than a military funeral organized by the IRA, then the Gardaí would give them every assistance. She told the Gardaí that she wouldn't need their assistance. The hearse was stoned by Protestant activists as it drove from Enniskillen to the house, where her son lay in an open coffin in an adjoining room until the burial, the house being open to those who wanted to come and express their sympathy and solidarity.

Her husband came in, having been out working on their small farm. He was older than she, a thin man, watchful, his gaze hard and somewhat ironic. He was amused at the visitor. He didn't want to talk about particulars, he was interested in history, in how things had come about. He was amused at my interest in the hiring fairs, and dismissed any sentimental views I had on the subject. Some of those hired had been treated very well by their Protestant masters, so much so that they had come to inherit the farms on which they worked. He knew of several such cases, he said.

He talked about various plantations from the sixteenth century onwards, exactly when the landlords had come to certain places, when the population had shifted. Very few families had kept the Republican flame alight after the Civil War ended, he said. Most people had been content to settle down. It was left to a few. A few families, most of them over the border in the South. If only the British had known this in 1969 and 1970, he said, that there were only a dozen or so IRA activists. If they had interned those people, and left everyone else alone, things would have taken a different course.

It was from this house in 1957 that several IRA men had set out to attack Brookeborough RUC Station. Two of them, Sean South and Feargal O'Hanlon, were killed in the attack, giving rise to a huge wave of sympathy in the South, even though the border campaign of the 1950s had no support in general. The attack also resulted in two of the most potent Irish ballads, 'Sean South of Garryowen', a rabble-rousing come-all-ye, and Dominic Behan's 'The Patriot Game', a more ironic and bitter tune:

> Come all ye young rebels and list while I sing
> For the love of one's country is a terrible thing
> It banishes fear with the speed of a flame
> And makes us all part of the Patriot Game.

As he talked about history and the past, his wife began to rummage in the corner of the room. I looked over and saw she had a photograph album in her hand. She leaned over and gave it to me. It had a sort of chocolate-box kitten on the cover. I opened it. The first few pages contained photographs of Seamus McElwain's funeral, ordinary, standard-size colour photographs, the sort people take on their holidays. They were just of faces in a crowd, a coffin, priests. I noticed one of his young brothers sitting on a chair in the corner watching me as I turned the pages. The father kept talking, wondering why no one had written about how his son was killed in cold blood, why there had been no investigation. Towards the end of the album there were photographs of Seamus McElwain in his coffin. I didn't want to look at them, but I found myself examining his dead face, which seemed to have a bruise or a mark on the left-hand side. He was dark, good-looking, young. I turned the pages and there were more. I closed the book and gave it back to his mother.

Tea was brought in, and chicken sandwiches. One of the daughters was in charge of making sure we had enough to eat. Each time I finished a sandwich, they insisted I had another. The father went out of the room for a while and then came back in.

'Niall Tóibín,' he said. 'That's a good one.' He laughed.

'No, Colm Tóibín is my name. Niall Tóibín is an actor. He's no relation.'

'I'd say you're a bit of an actor too,' he said. His eyes fixed on me, half amused, half ferocious. He grinned at me.

A few months later, there would be another split in Sinn Fein over whether or not the party would continue to abstain from the Dáil, the southern Parliament. This man would take the losing side, the unpopular path, siding with Ruairi O'Brádaigh against Gerry Adams in a dramatic vote in Dublin. Adams won the right to take seats in the Dáil, in Dublin.

The mother talked about relations in America, how they had offered to take Seamus and put him through college and get him away from all this; they were rich. But he decided not to go, to stay here and fight for his country instead. It was funny, she said, they never contacted the family when he was killed.

It was getting dark. I stood at the door looking out at the

bleak land, which stretched out for miles in front of the house; the dull half-light was made duller by the drizzle. There was no sign of another house for miles. The father and mother came to the door and we looked out at the night coming down early now that the summer was nearly over.

10

The Road to Darkley

I went back to Monaghan and the next day hitched a lift to Roslea, having checked the map and made up my mind to walk northwards to Fivemiletown and the Clogher Valley.

It was only when the British soldier was going through my bags in the village of Roslea, that I understood why I had chosen this route; it was remote. I was unlikely to meet anyone, I was unlikely to hear any stories of killing, revenge, or grief. I now possessed an Ordnance Survey map, which was even more useless than the Michelin map I had been using previously. This map had too many roads, the other one had too few. In the face of such a plethora of roads it was hard to know where to go, so I followed my nose and went in the direction I thought was north. One thing was sure: the little river Finn had made another appearance, innocent-looking, brown, apparently directionless, it had come back to haunt me, and I crossed over it warily. I was in the South now, having walked along a track from the North. The road was uphill all the way.

There were two new houses being built as I passed, one exactly on the site of an old house, the gable wall of the old house still standing. The second house had an excellent view of the countryside around, but the main windows were looking out on to the road. I came to a T-junction and once more in front of me, as though I were a spiked stick being led in search of water, was the lazy Finn, doing another casual twist and turn. I checked the map to ensure that this was the last time I would see it.

A man on a tractor passed me; he kept looking behind at me, as though I were a ghost, as if to make sure I was still there. The fields were full of rushes; the further uphill I went, the bleaker it became. A big mongrel dog came running out after me barking and yelping. Soon its owner emerged, a man in his fifties who

called the dog off. He was puzzled at my presence; not many
people came along this way, he said. I told him I was walking to
Fivemiletown. It was a long way, he said. The border was closed,
but I could probably get across by foot, he told me. There was
another crossing, but the road had been cratered in several places
and it was now almost completely impassable.

The road narrowed even further as a light mist started to come
down. There was a pine forest now on either side of the road. I
passed over the white 'X' painted on the road for helicopters to
see that this was where the United Kingdom of Great Britain and
Northern Ireland began. Soon the road petered out, and the old
familiar spikes came into sight, my old friends, sticking up towards
the sky from an ugly misshapen mass of concrete in a metal casing.
Several abandoned cars lay around, rusting. There was, for a good
distance, unrelieved muck. After the first spikes came a huge crater
followed by more concrete and more spikes.

On the other side of these impediments stood an abandoned
house. I had to walk on to the verge to try and remove the muck
from my shoes. I met two forestry workers who told me that
there was a turn ahead which led back into the South, the road
blocked by more spikes, craters and concrete. Fivemiletown was
a good walk still, but I had no choice but to persevere, as there
were a number of hotels there where I could rest my feet and get
shelter from the mist which was coming down harder. As the
afternoon went on it grew cold, with hints of winter. There was
no traffic on the road.

I went to bed as soon as I checked into the hotel in Fivemiletown, and slept for several hours. When I woke up I had a meal,
a few drinks, a walk up and down the dreary main street, whose
hidden secrets I left dark and unearthed, and then I went back to
bed where I slept soundly until morning.

After breakfast the next morning I looked at the map once
more, discovered that the mountain I had walked over was Slieve
Beagh, and determined to walk over it again, but this time in an
easterly direction towards Emyvale, Glaslough and Armagh. The
main road was busy; cars went by at high speed, and I wanted to
get on to a by-road as soon as I could. It was a cloudy day, but
the clouds were soft, and it was warm.

The Union Jack flew over the Clogher Valley Free Presbyterian Church, part of Ian Paisley's empire. I turned right and began to climb once more, unsure of my route, the Michelin and the Ordnance Survey map contradicted each other, and neither seemed to correspond with the actual terrain. I passed by three men who were standing in a barn looking intently at a cow's behind, one of them holding the tail up to give them a better view.

I came to Kell Methodist Church, and I asked the man who was painting the outside if he knew the way to the border. I told him I was walking. He said he hadn't been near the border for years, but he thought if I kept climbing I would find a crossing I could pass on foot. The sun began to shine. A woman watched me from a window, and moved to another window, and then another window in her new bungalow, looking out all the time, observing me. I could see the concern and fear in her face.

The forest then began again. There was a sign announcing Fardross Forest and a river walk, which was a relief after the hard asphalt of the road. I crossed a wooden bridge and lay down on a bench for some time, before continuing on my way. There was nobody around. I emerged from the forest walk on to another road. When I went up a bit higher I could see the whole Augher–Clogher Valley down below. There was a watchtower on one of the adjacent hills.

I asked the first man I met about the watchtower. He told me there was an old landlord buried there, who had ordered the tower to be built as his tomb, the view was so spectacular, with so many different mountains on the horizon. It was a good place for your bones to rest, the man said. However, the landlord had been dug up, and the bones scattered by people hunting for treasure. Rumour had it that the lead coffin contained whiskey and a gold watch. Were the treasure hunters local people? I asked. No, it was the American army. Did he mean the British army? I asked. No, he said, the American army, billeted here during the war, the Second World War, known as the Emergency in the South. Local people had fooled them into thinking that there was treasure in the landlord's tomb, and after a few drinks one night they had gone up the hill and opened the coffin.

He pointed out a couple making hay in a field below where we were standing. They seemed to be working hard. 'Strange what some people have to do to get by,' he said. The man was eighty-five and the woman was in her seventies, he said. They had one son who was married, but he had left the area.

It was a Catholic area, he said, but still no one went South. The South was expensive. The life here was hard in the winter, he said, especially when there was snow. Sometimes it didn't melt for weeks, and houses would be cut off. Cars couldn't come up, and he remembered that years ago in the winter, if someone died the coffin would have to be carried down the mountain to the valley. The land was bad, and the grants for drainage, which had been as high as ninety-five per cent, were now as low as twenty per cent. The army, he said, never came by road. They flew by helicopter. 'I'd say they'd give a fellow like you a good drilling,' he said, smiling at the thought of it. He warned me that he had been told that the army was about the place today. I should watch out for them.

The land moved from bogland to land where nothing grew. Signs that this was a game sanctuary appeared at regular intervals. Gorse appeared, and then heather. There were no houses or signs of habitation. The day became fine, the sun hot, the white clouds hovered on the horizon. Sometimes over the next few miles the land improved, and once I met a farmer and his son working in a field, saving hay. The border, they said, was just a mile away.

There was a light sound from the wind, a few hills and bare fields, patches of purple heather. I kept feeling that I was near the sea, that beyond the hill were sand dunes and the ocean. Then I saw the soldiers straight ahead, the first one lying flat on his belly pointing a rifle at some target in the nearest hill. He turned towards me, asking me for identification. I showed him my press card, and he told me to walk ahead to where the next soldier would want to talk to me.

The next soldier was friendly. I told him I was walking into the South, and he seemed interested in this, as though he would like to come as well. It was lovely here, he said, he liked this part of the world. It resembled the Falklands, he said, these colours, the bleak landscape, the heather, the quietness. In the Falklands, however, there were no trees at all, he said. He had liked it there as well; one day he went windsurfing in the South Atlantic, and that was really exciting; it was beautiful – he was followed by dolphins.

I could tell from the accent that he was Welsh. He had been away from his wife and kids for three months now, he said; he missed them, but would be home in a few weeks. Then he would be back for a longer stretch; he would be able to bring them with him, and they would have their own accommodation here in the North. He showed me his map, making sure that none of his comrades could see what he was doing. The map was incredibly detailed, every house, every field, every road, carefully denoted and described. It would be impossible to go wrong with such a map. Different colours made everything clear. He laughed when I explained my plight with maps. I showed him my Michelin and my Ordnance Survey, and he shook his head in wonder at how out-of-date they were. His was the map I should have, he said.

I left him and crossed a field which had once been a road, but was now overgrown, to get to the South, almost slipping a few times in the muck. A herd of cattle began to take an inordinate amount of interest in me as I progressed. It didn't take me long to spot the bull among them nosing his way towards me. I wasn't far from the road, which began at a nearby house, and I decided the best thing to do was run. The muck was too much, however, and I fell after a few yards, covering my hands and trouser knees in slime and muck. I looked behind; the bull was still gazing at me, but more in astonishment and incomprehension than in anger or with menace. I picked myself up, and walked casually towards the road, making sure with regular glances that the bull was keeping his distance. I tried to wipe the muck from my hands and shoes on the grass, but the grass was damp. And so I had to put up with the drying muck as I walked along in the warm sunshine.

There wasn't a sound. I passed by a few houses which seemed to be inhabited, but there was no sign of life, no cars, no faces at the windows, no children playing. I passed by an abandoned primary school.

When I came to a crossroads I found myself close to Scotstown again, where I had seen Seamus McElwain's parents, but I turned left towards Emyvale. As I walked along, more and more life appeared in the shape of cars, houses, new bungalows, children. A boy detached himself from a group outside a row of houses, and asked me if I was a foot patrol. This seemed a good enough description of me, so I told him I was, and he went back to his companions and reported the news.

I went into the first pub I saw in Emyvale, where I devoured several sandwiches and several pints of lager shandy, then went to telephone Desmond Leslie, the owner of Castle Leslie, which was about three miles away. I had been to the house once before, and he had given me a grand tour of the locality, so I wondered if he was free to repeat some of this, or offer some additions. He suggested I go to Glaslough, the village adjoining the Leslie estate, establish myself in the local hotel, and telephone him then.

There were boats out on Emylough in the calm, warm evening. Signs of bad weather were apparent, however, in the deep marks and cuts which the tractors and harvesters had made in the fields, still soft and soggy after one of the worst summers in living memory. The hotel in Glaslough was positioned at one of the gates to Castle Leslie. I left my rucksack upstairs, had a drink in the bar, ordered dinner and rang Desmond Leslie once more. He was busy that evening, he said, but agreed to see me at eleven o'clock the next morning.

There was a time when the Leslies, who came here in 1664, owned eighty thousand acres, employed thirty-three indoor staff and twenty-eight gardeners. They owned land as far west as Station Island on Lough Derg. Desmond's father, Sir Shane Leslie, wrote a book on the history of the island. The family was always writing books. Jonathan Swift, when he stayed in the house, wrote in the guest book:

> Glaslough with rows of books upon its shelves
> Written by the Leslies all about themselves.

Although the family fortunes declined after the First World War, the Leslies still managed to hold on to the big house, Castle Leslie, some of the land, and a great deal of the bookishness and eccentricity inherited from their aristocratic forebears. Desmond composed celestial music, and had written a bestselling volume on UFOs. After I banged on the big door the next morning at eleven, I had to wait for some time before Desmond opened it dramatically, looking like a cross between an owl and an oak tree; he was tall and gaunt; his big, haunting eyes gazed out from thick spectacles; his thick greying hair was long and curled up at the end; he was wearing a huge brown dressing gown, like a shroud; his voice with its elaborate, almost exaggerated English vowel sounds seemed like something from a vampire movie. He talked slowly, watching carefully for the effect of each word on his listener.

On my last visit to the estate he had shown us the redwoods, and the Douglas firs, which rose to between 180 and 200 feet, and the ice house, as well as the walled garden he now rented out to a local man.

'This,' he had said, pointing to a lane, 'was once the country road, but we didn't want the proles coming too close, so we had it moved.' I remembered how he had said 'proles', and how he watched me to see how I would react.

The proles were all around now, their houses in Glaslough were listed to prevent them making unsightly improvements ('hideous picture windows' was Desmond's phrase) to the village built in stone by the Leslies for their workers. The locals made a good living out of the smuggling industry; those who were pre-pared to take the small risk involved in carting farm machinery, spare parts for cars, alcohol, tobacco and electrical goods across the border, or those who conveyed animals across in the dead of night, could make a lot of money without much work. As we passed by a young local, Desmond pointed him out, saying that every time he went into the North he was arrested and accused of terrorist activity because of his name, even though he had no involvement whatsoever with the IRA, thus forcing Desmond to drive up to the police station where the youth was held and vouch for his innocence.

There were three estates beside each other: the Leslie estate, whose boundary ran along the border; the estate of Lord Caledon in the North; and Tynan Abbey, the home of Sir Norman Stronge, the former speaker of the Parliament of Northern Ireland at Stormont, who was killed by the IRA along with his son James in 1979; the house was burned to the ground.

The Leslies had never had much connection with the Caledons. Desmond thought they were probably very dull. In the eighteenth century they had purchased Bishop Percy's library.

'Lord Caledon told the farm steward to go and buy it. No one knew what was in it until my father went to look,' Desmond said. It included a first folio of a Marlowe play, with Shakespeare's autograph as well, and an Audubon book of bird paintings. There was a time, however, when there were four Caledon boys and four Leslie boys at Eton simultaneously; they used to travel to Dublin together on the old railway line. They used to refuse to buy tickets, according to Desmond, 'to the consternation of the ticket collector'.

We walked through Castle Leslie itself, through the old ornate living rooms, to the servants' quarters where the Leslies now spent most of their time. Desmond began to muse about the old days when 'the junior servants waited on the senior ones', when the Duke of Devonshire's valet took precedence over Lord Brookeborough's valet, when there was a housekeeper's room.

Now his wife was working at the sink, as Desmond and myself drank instant coffee from mugs. His daughter ran a riding school on the estate, and was about to celebrate her birthday. Desmond left me at the kitchen table to go through a brochure on the house and its history, while he went to his study where he was writing a long novel, an 'upmarket *Dynasty*', a 'lovely romp', on 'a little word processor'.

Mother and daughter, meanwhile, stood behind me discussing the guests for the daughter's birthday party; a list of who would and who wouldn't be invited was followed by a judicious consideration of the squirearchy of the area. I listened to all this attentively as I read about the old primeval forest which still stood inside the demesne walls, around which 'an estimated half million rooks' were known to fly at certain times.

Soon Desmond came back and inquired if I needed anything more. There was a good history of Monaghan I could consult in the county library, he said. I replied that I would like to look around the house again, if he didn't mind. I was tired. I had slept for more than ten hours the previous night, which made me feel exhausted, like I needed ten more hours of the same deep sleep. I longed to sit at one of the windows of Castle Leslie and look out for a while before I started walking again, drink in all the opulence, the legacy of centuries, wallow in the spoils of eighty thousand acres. Desmond told me I could look around all I liked, escorted me to the room beside his study, and left me there, while he went into his study and firmly closed the door.

I walked towards the window, feeling somewhat sheepish and uncomfortable, and thinking that I should perhaps make my way quietly out of the house, rather than cause any further inconvenience, when a door opened and a man came in and stood in front of me. He looked like a ghost. He was rather surprised to see me. He introduced himself as Desmond's brother. I wondered if this wasn't some elaborate joke.

'How do you do?' he said to me. I explained that Desmond had told me I could wander around the house.

'Good,' he said. It was hard to think of anything else to say. We looked at each other, until I asked him which was the way to the front door. He politely pointed me towards the door he had just come in.

'Goodbye,' I said to him.

'Goodbye,' he said. I opened the big front door, and walked back down the avenue to the village, where I collected my rucksack and went on my way.

Desmond had told me that if I followed the demesne wall I would come to the border, which I could cross by foot, and then go on to Caledon, Tynan, Middletown. On the right as I walked along were the remnants of the old railway, part of the Great Northern Railway system which once had lines running through the North, but now confined itself to the Dublin to Belfast route, the rest having closed down in 1959. I passed a beautiful old stone railway bridge. The Leslie demesne wall was still reasonably intact.

Just as the road began to deteriorate and the abandoned houses began to appear, the roadblock came into view. I crossed over into the North and walked along for a while before I was accosted

by a woman who was coming towards me. Was I a British MP?
she wanted to know. I told her I wasn't. Far from it, I added.
They were expecting a group of MPs she said, who were doing
a tour of the area. The roadblock, she said, was there only a
fortnight. Before then, the road had been open. There were two
men shot on this road by the IRA, she told me, one in 1979,
one in 1982.

'One was shot around that bad corner,' she said, pointing to
the road ahead. 'The other was shot while going to feed his cattle.'
One of them worked for Lord Caledon. Both were in the UDR.
Lord Caledon's estate was big, she thought, but Sir Norman
Stronge, who was shot with his son, hadn't more than a few
hundred acres. I asked her who now owned the Stronge's land.
Some of the family had inherited it, she said, but they didn't use
it any more, they lived elsewhere and they leased it out. Some of
the local Republicans had bid for parcels of the land, she said,
and had spent their time cutting down trees on it and abusing it.
The rest of it was leased out to responsible farmers. There was a
movement now, she said, to stop the Republicans renewing their
lease, to outbid them. A lot of the local Protestants were upset
by what had happened.

She spoke freely, without any suspicion. But she would tell
me nothing about herself: neither where she lived, nor her name.
As we talked a large white car drove down the lane towards us.
'Look at the arch smuggler,' she said. 'Up and down here all day.'
She folded her arms and gazed at the driver of the approaching
car, making no secret of her contempt. I pointed out to her that
the road was blocked; but, she told me, a short simple detour
allowed access to the South. The roadblock was cosmetic. 'Look
at him,' she said. 'But he won't go over now with you here.
Look at him stalling.' The man had stopped his car at the border.

'Watch him now,' she said. 'He'll turn back.' She was right.
After a short wait, he turned the car and drove slowly back
towards us, keeping his head down as he passed. I asked her what
he was smuggling, but she refused to say. She laughed, saying that
the white car was only one of many.

When I came to the river Blackwater a few hundred yards
beyond the border, they were building a new bridge. I walked

through a wood before I came to a paved road which led to Middletown. I was now in County Armagh. Traces of the old railway system appeared constantly, like severed limbs. The road was overhung with trees. The entrance to Tynan Abbey was imposing, like the entrance to a huge castle. The land here was good. I passed the first field of barley I had seen in these regions.

I was stopped by the army in Middletown, travelling in groups of four as usual, and one of them gave me directions to Clontibret, which was the village Peter Robinson and his supporters had marched on earlier in the summer. None of the roads he suggested was marked on my map. I had abandoned the Ordnance Survey map on the basis that it was better to carry a map with a few roads marked than a map with too many, some of which didn't exist. I had a drink in Middletown, the barman assuring me that Robinson must have had assistance from the locals to weave his way along these lonely roads. He and his supporters couldn't have done it alone at night, they would have lost their way.

I walked through the village, where some of the shops were closed up, some of the houses abandoned, especially those close to the army checkpoint which would be hit by IRA mortar bombs later in the year. The town gave the army protection. The few miles from here to the border was no-go land, with no checkpoints at the border itself. The road was wide, its surface smooth as glass. There was a sign up advertising a hi-fi shop down a side road, for those who wanted to smuggle radios or three-in-ones into the South without having to drive through a British army checkpoint.

I turned down the side road as instructed by the British soldier. To my right in the distance I could see the cathedral of Monaghan town under the grey sky. Soon I came to a roadblock, which no longer functioned effectively. It was a huge chunk of concrete with the usual spikes, which blocked a road, but a new road had been built to the side of it, eating into a field, thus making nonsense of the concrete. I was in the South now, on one of the maze of small roads which Robinson and his gang had used to visit Clontibret in the middle of the night.

Further along, as I came near the turning which would take

me down into Clontibret, I met a man who was standing at his door. He was in his sixties. He didn't think it would rain, he said. When I asked him about Robinson he said he didn't know which way he had come. He didn't like the idea of Robinson and his friends, and he added that he didn't think there was any future in this part of the country anyway. 'When love goes out of a place, there's nothing left,' he said. 'The young people are all brought up on bombs and guns.' The British army had come to his door once, wanting to search his house. They knew they were in the South, he said, and threatened to shoot him if he didn't let them in, but when he was adamant that he wouldn't cooperate with them, they went back over the border to the North.

He pointed to a place north of Monaghan, and told me a story about how his father had been taken by a Protestant into a solicitor's office one day over thirty years ago in the town. His father had been fed several whiskeys. His father wasn't used to drink and had agreed, the man told me, to sign a document which eventually led to him losing his small farm and house. His father was dead. So was the Protestant. But the Protestant's son was alive; he knew where the man lived, he said, and before he died he was going to put that man's house to the torch. His tone was matter of fact, his voice low and confiding.

'Contentment,' he mused. 'All you need is contentment.' I stood there and listened. He gave me the name of the man whose house he was going to burn.

As I turned right and proceeded down the hill which would take me to Clontibret, I met a farmer with a herd of cows and asked him if this was the way Peter Robinson had come to Clontibret. He didn't know, he said. As I walked on, with the whole of North Monaghan stretched out before me down below, a blue van passed, braked suddenly, started moving again, braked again and went on. A few minutes later the same van came up the hill in the opposite direction. I didn't like the look on the driver's face. Over to my left a helicopter hovered in the late afternoon sky, reminding me that the North was close at hand, and that I was near South Armagh. I continued walking down the hill. The van approached again, moving slowly past me and then stopping. Suddenly the driver reversed until he was level with me. He pulled down the window.

'What do you want to know about Peter Robinson for?' he asked.

'I'm a reporter,' I said. 'I'm retracing his steps.' It sounded ridiculous.

'Could you account for yourself if a patrol came out?' he asked.

'I could,' I replied with as much certainty as I could muster.

'What are you doing with that?' he asked, pointing to my rucksack.

'I'm walking, my clothes are in there,' I answered, beginning to wonder why I was answering this fellow's questions at all.

'A funny way for a reporter to travel,' he said. I didn't reply; I could think of nothing to say. He took another look at me, making it clear how much he disapproved of my general bearing, started up the van and drove off. As I walked down the hill I thought of all the smart answers I could have given him.

As soon as I reached a junction I turned right for Clontibret, and noticed a Garda patrol car coming towards me; a plain-clothes detective's car came behind me. They both stopped, blocking the road. The detective got out and one of the two Gardaí pulled down the window of the car. It occurred to me that the detective might be armed. Where was I going? they asked.

'Did a man telephone you saying I was asking about Peter Robinson?' I enquired. They assented. I told them what I was doing. I gave them my name and identification, explaining how I had been harassed by a fellow in a blue van.

'I hope you're going to write about how quickly we had you under surveillance,' the Garda in the passenger's seat said and grinned. I assured him that I would. He told me that one of the two Gardaí who was injured on the night of the Robinson invasion was back at work, but the other was still in hospital with a back injury.

The Garda patrol car drove off; the detective turned his car and drove after them.

I went down to the main Monaghan–Castleblayney road, and walked on towards Clontibret. The cars were speeding, some of them doing up to ninety miles an hour. The road was new; a big sign announced 'This Project Is Being Aided By The European Regional Development Fund'. It was a dangerous road to walk on; almost no provision had been made for the pedestrian, and I felt that if one of these cars even touched me, it would be the end, I would be finished. Several lorries went by, carrying hay from the South to the North, which was still suffering from the bad harvest. I was still interested in Robinson's path, even though no one wanted to talk about it, so I went up to the first man I came to in the village of Clontibret and asked the question: 'Is this the way Robinson came in?' But he didn't answer. 'He should never have been let in,' he simply said. 'They should have shot the bastard.'

In the pub, which was empty, the woman behind the bar told me that she had slept right through the event. She had missed everything, all the shouting and screaming of the protestors.

They had painted slogans on the walls of the school and the Garda station, she said. I should look at both buildings for signs of new paint. Robinson was due in court in Ballybay, just six miles away, in a few days, having already made a court appearance at Dundalk. He had brought his supporters with him to Dundalk, and they had been attacked by local youths. A crate of petrol bombs thrown out of a window had almost killed several people. Robinson and his friends went back to the North. The woman behind the bar hoped he wouldn't bring too many supporters to Ballybay. There would be trouble if he did, she said. The army and the Gardaí would be out in force.

They were still painting the school house as I passed by. There was nowhere to stay in Clontibret; the next resting place was Castleblayney, a good seven miles away. I hated walking on this main road; it was, anyway, getting dark, so I started to hitch a lift, and was soon picked up by a commercial traveller and deposited in the main street of Castleblayney.

Castleblayney was the centre of the country and western music industry in Ireland, whose high priest, Tony Loughman, still had a pub in the town. Loughman managed all the great local acts, such as Big Tom and Susan McCann, who played to huge audiences in dance halls all over the country. But I was too tired now for songs about love, honour and adultery sung in American accents in Castleblayney on a Friday night, so after a few drinks I went to bed.

The next morning I set out from Castleblayney to Keady in the North. It was another dull day. Hay was still being brought North on lorries. The petrol pumps on the outskirts of the town were closed completely, they had become a monument to days gone by, with no future use. There was a large house with two garages at a crossroads surrounded by bogland; a balcony off the main bedroom had a Spanish-style balustrade, French windows downstairs leading on to the bog and columns in every possible quarter. Desmond Leslie looked down on all this modern Irish architecture from the heights of his castle, referring to the new bungalows as the 'gombeen style', a gombeen being a slang term for a Catholic money-man or shopkeeper in the nineteenth century. This more elaborate design, which took its bearing from *Dallas* and *The High Chapparal*, he called 'the high gombeen style'.

I was tired. The watery grey sky was getting to me; the lack of sunshine was making me morose. As I came out of a small country shop, having bought a bar of chocolate and a bottle of lemonade, I saw a Garda car driving out of a side road, with an inspector in the front seat and several senior Garda officers in the back. This was followed by a state car, reserved for government ministers. In the back seat of this car sat Alan Dukes, the then Southern Minister for Justice. He glared at me for a moment, and I glared back at him. He was the last person in the world I expected to see on a Saturday morning. A couple of minutes later the entire entourage drove back again. I waved at Dukes as he went by, but he didn't bat an eyelid. Within a year he would replace Garret FitzGerald as leader of the Fine Gael party.

The man at the customs post told me when I arrived at the border that the three cars had come up the road, stopped for a second, and turned, it seemed that they just wanted to look at the border.

Dukes had flown in by helicopter that morning, he said, to Carrickmacross, and was looking at border crossings. In that case, he was looking at nothing. The only sign of the border here was the southern customs post. The British army had moved their post right back into the town of Keady where they stopped all cars. Anyone could drive through here without any difficulty. If the army had a post out here they'd be slaughtered, the customs man said. This was Provo territory, where the Provisional IRA was strong.

Provo territory was quiet as I went through it on the way to Keady. I had been told that there was a hotel in Keady, and I determined to settle down there for a few days and rest myself. I dreamed as I walked along of a warm hotel bedroom, a hot bath, roast lamb, pints of Guinness, hot whiskeys, long sleeps, no exertion of any description. I passed the army checkpoint in Keady without any trouble and discovered, as soon as I asked, that there was no hotel in Keady. It had closed down. I went to a pub and wondered what to do.

The owner of the pub and his wife brought me to the door and showed me where the market house and library had once stood. They were bombed after Bloody Sunday in 1972, when thirteen unarmed demonstrators were shot dead by the British army in Derry. There had been a big march this year in Keady on 9 August, which had caused a lot of damage in the town. As the pub owner began to tell me about it, he realized that it would be better if he drove me around the town and showed me what had happened. We went outside and got into the car. Most of Keady was Catholic, he said, but there was one completely Prot-estant housing estate called Annvale Gardens but known locally as Paisley Park, in honour of the DUP leader. A few people stood and watched us as we drove around the estate.

The parade on 9 August had come from Paisley Park, and sought to make its way into the centre of the town, but the police had blocked the road with Land Rovers. The crowd had broken the windows of all the Catholic shops on the street; the Protestant shops remained unmolested. The parade was then re-routed towards the Orange Hall outside the town, and the crowd broke the windows in the Catholic housing estate. The bar owner himself lived in this estate; people were very frightened, he said.

Back in the bar, I asked him about Darkley, the place where the INLA (the Irish National Liberation Army, a more militant, more gung-ho paramilitary force than the IRA) went into a prayer meeting in a small country meeting house and opened fire on a Sunday afternoon in November 1983, killing three men and injuring others. The pastor still lived there, I was assured; his name was Bob Bain. The bar owner gave me directions to his house.

I was tempted to go back to Castleblayney and telephone him, but I had come this far and it was just a few miles down the road. I started walking again, passing an army patrol, edging their way carefully through a housing estate at the top of the town. I took several wrong turns, until I was finally put on the right road.

I had to ask directions several times, as the area was full of crossroads and T-junctions; each time I asked for Bob Bain's house I was met with puzzled looks, but when I said he was the pastor whose congregation had been attacked, they understood, and directed me to his house. As soon as I walked into his yard I was surrounded by dogs, who continued barking as they circled me, preventing me from getting any further. Eventually, a woman in her fifties with grey hair, tied in a bun at the back of her head, came out and stood some distance from me. I told her I was looking for Bob Bain; she said he wasn't in. 'Are you born again?' I asked her. This wasn't the question I had meant to ask, but it came out like that. Her face changed completely. She smiled almost girlishly, and pushed a wisp of hair back from her face. 'Yes, I am,' she said. There was a glow in her eyes as she looked at me.

I asked her if they still had a service every Sunday in their church. They did, she said, but not as many people came to the service since the shooting, people were afraid. They had lost a lot of their congregation. Did she think, I asked, that I would be allowed to come to the service? I would have to ask her husband; it was best to telephone him. She gave me the number and I wrote it down.

I asked her where the meeting house was, and she directed me to a place some distance from her house. It was a steep climb. The words 'Fuck The IRA' were written across the road. The surrounding hills were covered in trees. The place where the congregation met was a wooden building with 'Mountain Lodge Pentecostal Assembly' written up outside. The windows were covered with wire. It was built on a ridge. There was a clear view for miles on the other side, to Armagh and beyond. The border was just half a mile down the road.

When I walked back down the hill, I saw a lorry coming and I put out my thumb. I was in luck; the driver was going to Newry. He dropped me outside the town where the lorries congregated, putting their documents in order before going South. I decided I would hitchhike for five minutes and if I failed to get a lift I would walk back into Newry. The second car stopped, I was in luck once more, and it brought me as far as Dundalk.

When I had found a hotel I rang Bob Bain at the number his wife had given me.

'There are two questions I want to ask you,' he said as soon as I told him what I wanted.

'What are they?' I asked.

'Firstly are you a member of the INLA?' I explained that I wasn't, that I was merely a reporter who wanted to attend a service with his congregation. I tried to do this as vehemently as I could, but he remained calm, and when I had replied he said that he just needed to check that, because if I were a member of the INLA he would be in trouble. Did I understand that? he asked. He seemed to feel that it would be quite normal for a member of the INLA to telephone him to ask to attend a service.

'The second question is this: What religion are you?' he asked. I hesitated for a moment and then answered: 'I'm a Catholic.'

'Well,' he said, 'you know that you have to be born again.'

'You mean to get into your service?' I asked.

'No, for your life,' he answered.

He told me to come to the three o'clock service the following day, and he would make sure that I was looked after.

The next day I got a taxi from Dundalk. Because of roadblocks we had to do several detours, one of which took us past the memorial to twelve-year-old Majella O'Hara, marking the place where ten years earlier she was shot dead by British soldiers.

There were several cars parked outside 'Mountain Lodge Pentecostal Assembly'. As I paid the taxi driver I could hear the sound of music. I stood at the back of the hall for a while as a small organ, a piano, drums and an accordion were being played.

The man I took to be Bob Bain was at the top of the room trying to get the few people who had arrived to sing louder. The chorus went: 'Once and for all'. He beat his fist in the air in time to the music. 'I love to hear someone starting up again. When you're going to Markethill or Portadown, strike up a chorus and sing all the way,' he said. He was an old-fashioned preacher, in a place with a tradition of great preachers going back two centuries. Being born again was nothing new in the North. In 1859, for example, there was a Great Revival in which a hundred thousand people were born again.

The long room began to fill up now, this Sunday afternoon. Most of the congregation looked like ordinary members of a farming community. All the women wore hats. There was a lanky young man across from me who was standing up, with his arms spread out. Except for this, and the accordion and drums at the top of the room, it could have been a small congregation at prayer on a Sunday anywhere in Ireland.

Mr Bain had nodded at me when I came in and pointed to a seat which he urged me to sit in. Now, as he came down the long room to close the door, he winked at me as he passed. The wink seemed planned to reassure me that everything was as he said it would be. He was a bustling little man, full of enthusiasm.

When he went back up to the top of the room, he told the thirty or so people who had arrived that there was a stranger among them, and a few people turned and smiled at me. I was interested, he said, in what had happened in 1983, how three of their congregation were killed by those 'who had done their utmost to kill everyone. The men who did it, if they're still unsaved, they need to be saved.' This congregation, he said, had been seen on television all over the world; letters, more than eight thousand letters, had come from people all over the world. What they wanted to do now, he said, was sing the hymn that they were singing when the killers came in. Hymn 171. They found the hymn in their books.

The music began. Mr Bain took out a tambourine and played it while they sang:

Have you been to Jesus for the cleansing power?
Are you washed in the blood of the lamb?
Are you fully trusting in his grace this hour?
Are you washed in the blood of the lamb?

They had three verses sung, and were halfway through the fourth when the gunmen came to the outside door and shot the three men who were standing there. It was twenty past six. The inner door was closed. The gunmen didn't open it, but tried to shoot through it and then went outside and stood shooting through the thin wooden walls of the building. They shot low, because the congregation were lying on the floor, wounding a number of people. They were wearing red masks.

There was a plaque on the wall to the three men:

In Loving Memory of Our Three Elders William Harold Browne, John Victor Cunningham, Richard Samuel David Wilson Who Were Killed By Terrorists In This Church Service. Sadly Missed By All. Who Shall Separate Us From The Love of Christ? Romans 8v:35. Erected by Mountain Lodge Pentecostal Church, Darkley.

When the hymn was over, they got down to the real business of the day. Two women had come to preach to them: the first was in her early sixties, she wore glasses; the other was at least twenty years younger. The women seemed to tour such churches all over the North. As the older woman began to speak, the British army appeared outside.

'All my life I was a Roman Catholic,' she said. 'I believed everything that my church taught. I became alcoholic; the circumstances don't matter. After years of drinking and smoking and drug-taking I was still a devout Roman Catholic. I used to stagger to Mass.

'After another year drinking I got worse. Times I didn't know whether it was day or night. I had ulcers. I couldn't start the day without whiskey to anaesthetize the pain. One morning after the children had gone out to school I didn't really want to live any longer. I poured out a drink and tablets. I was ready to die when I heard a voice saying: "Turn inwards to your soul and you will find me there." '

Her voice grew louder and more exultant:

'Jesus saved me that morning. He saved my body and he saved my soul. I used to come out of confession confused and in misery. When I said "Help me" to the priest he would say, "Go home and try not to drink too much." The doctor said the same. I had nobody, and I turned to Jesus. Jesus Christ is the only hope this world has. Jesus is the only hope Ireland has. Jesus is my all; he's my everything. Think of the bullets that ripped through those walls. Time might be shorter than you think.'

As she began to sing in a contralto voice, the British army moved around the building. The other woman joined in the singing. The chorus was: 'That love can forgive, that love can forgive anything'. The second woman stood up to speak, praising the people in front of her who, after the shooting, could have said, We're not going to open up again. 'Praise God, you didn't,' she said. 'Is it possible,' she asked, 'to build a land again out of this rubble, this mess? It is possible by one means and one means only and that is the Gospel of the Lord. Jesus died for all men.

'I was brought up in the Presbyterian Church,' she said, 'and I didn't hear the Gospel until I was saved. Protestants are being told that Catholics are the enemy. Catholics are being told that Protestants are the enemy. The Devil is the enemy.'

She called on them to have courage and remain steadfast. 'There are far too many Evangeli-fish about; we need backbone,' she said. She had a serious illness, and had been to thirteen different doctors. 'I trusted in the Lord, do I need to tell you that he healed me? Jesus can heal!' There were cries of Amen! from the congregation.

The two women preachers sat down. Readings from the Bible were followed by hymns. People shouted up their favourite hymns and they were sung. A woman sitting near me told me afterwards that she had been baptized in this church just the previous Sunday with a number of others. The ceremony had taken place behind the church in a water tank. They believed in total immersion.

'Was it cold?' I asked her. 'It was surely,' she said, 'but it was worth it.'

Several people waited behind: those who were ill and wanted to be healed by Pastor Bain. They included a young girl who had an eye which was slightly crooked. From outside I could hear him shouting: 'I command the devil to take his dirty hands off these eyes.' I stood watching the army driving down the hill. The two women preachers waved goodbye to me.

When Bob Bain came out we walked around the hall until we faced north towards Armagh. I pointed to the Catholic cathedral jutting up out of the town.

'Would you like to have a church as big as that?' I asked him. He wouldn't, he said; what he had here was stronger and better, he was sure of that.

11

Surviving South Armagh

I came then in early September to Crossmaglen, famed in song and story. Everyone told me to be careful; this was South Armagh, you couldn't just casually walk around talking to people. The locals had good reason to be suspicious of strangers. There were, anyway, no hotels or guest houses in the area. I rang Sinn Fein headquarters in Belfast and spoke to someone there, told him what I wanted to do: live in an ordinary house in Crossmaglen and go about the area talking to people. The man in Belfast thought that it could be arranged; when I rang him back he gave me a number in Crossmaglen to telephone, and he put me in the hands of a local Sinn Fein man, Jim McAllister.

Crossmaglen was a large square with a number of streets running from it. The square was dominated by the British army post, behind which lay the army base. Army helicopters came and went, flying low over the roofs of the houses, their deafening engines a constant sound. The army sometimes patrolled the square, or the streets off the square, but sometimes they disappeared into the base and were not to be seen. Similarly, the helicopters sometimes ceased their comings and goings.

The Sinn Fein office in the main square was closed when I arrived in Crossmaglen. I had no idea where I was to be billeted, so I went into the local library and rummaged around.

I found a magazine which gave an account of various episodes in the history of South Armagh, including this view of the area by one Joshua Magee, coroner at Armagh assizes on 1 November 1847: 'The country around Newtownhamilton is mountainous. The people undereducated, wild and fierce in their disposition. The people are divided into two hostile factions, Orange and Catholic.' Five years later, the Deputy Inspector General of the

Police, Major Henry Browning wrote: 'Crossmaglen, I believe, is probably the worst part of the country.'

I left the library, and went once more in search of Jim McAllister, who was now sitting in the Sinn Fein office. He had found me lodging, he said. He was in his early forties, quick with words, his conversation full of bitter twists and ironic turns. He wrote poems, he said, and he showed me one of them, clearly typed. It was about being arrested by the British army and being taken by helicopter to the base in Bessbrook, across his world, his territory, the places he knew; which those who had arrested him would never know and had no claim to. The poem imagined a crash:

> And should my bones smash on Sturgan Brae
> Or bleach in Camlough waters, I'd be at home in my land
> The rest at map reference F 13, Sheet 3, South Armagh.

The most recent battle over whose land this was centred on a number of farms down the road, all of them close to the border. In the previous Sunday's *Observer* Mary Holland had written about Hugh O'Hanlon, a sheep farmer in Glasdrumman a few miles away, on whose land 'there now stands a tower of concrete and corrugated iron, supported by scaffolding and protected by sandbags and barbed wire. Across the road, a television camera has been perched on a pole to monitor the movements of passers-by. Gaping holes have been cut in the hedges and withered trees litter the fields. This is the latest in a line of fortified observation posts strung out across a vulnerable stretch of the border in South Armagh . . . When the army first arrived, Mr O'Hanlon asked a young soldier how long they would be needing his three fields. He was told: "We'll be here until the border goes and that won't be in your lifetime or mine." '

The moderate Catholic party, the SDLP, would cash in on this, and make statements, Jim McAllister said, but Sinn Fein's position was clear and logical: we don't just want these monstrosities out, we want the whole British apparatus, lock, stock and barrel, out. Behind him in his office were posters warning people not to speak to strangers. 'This Brit Could Be Standing Beside You' and 'Loose Talk Costs Lives' were the captions.

Jim brought me up through the square to his mother's house,

where we were fed, and from there to a housing estate at the side of the Gaelic football pitch, where he introduced me to my landlady, who lived in a three-bedroomed house with her young son. There was a small computer in my bedroom, the property of her son, who, she said, was curious to know if I had an interest in computers. When I had dropped my rucksack, Jim wanted to take me on a tour of the locality, and introduce me to local notables of the Republican persuasion.

We passed a leaning pylon, part of a North–South electricity scheme which had been consistently bombed by the IRA. There had never been any sectarian problem in Crossmaglen, Jim said, as we passed a small Protestant church; there were few Protestant families in the area.

So he wondered what the British were doing here, as we drove along. They weren't keeping the peace, as the place was perfectly peaceful, there was no trouble between Catholic and Protestant, neighbour and neighbour, as there was elsewhere. The war was between the locals and the British army. So what would happen if the British army withdrew? Peace, quiet, harmony, that's what would happen. So, what were they here for? Jim looked at me as though I might know. I said I had no idea.

There was a long tradition of dying for Ireland; the history of the Crossmaglen area was full of small, individual sacrifices. In every part of the area there were monuments to those who had died for Irish freedom. Sinn Fein and the IRA wanted to establish their roots in that long and emotional Irish tradition, to place their martyrs of the past sixteen years in the company of the executed leaders of the 1916 Rising, of the men shot in the War of Independence or the Civil War. Commemorations and monuments were of immense significance to them, as they were to the Unionists; Sunday after Sunday was spent at the graves of the dead, the young members of Sinn Fein attending as much as the old guard, who understood the importance of tradition.

Jim stopped at a huge monument in the village of Cullyhanna. I got out of the car and went over to look at it. It stood in the place of importance often reserved in an Irish village for a statue of the Virgin Mary. 'In Proud and Loving Memory of one of Ireland's noblest sons, Captain Michael McVerry, O/C First

Battalion South Armagh Brigade, Oglaigh na hEireann Born at
Cullyhanna, 1 December 1949, Killed in Action by British Forces
of Occupation at Keady RUC Barracks, 15 November 1973.'

How could they get permission to build a monument, here
in the North, to a man who had been killed so recently while
trying to blow up a police station? Jim shrugged. They didn't
look for permission. They just built it. 'The Department of
the Environment paid to build the wall,' he said, laughing. In the
South, the monuments were to those long dead; this was to a
man killed as recently as 1973. The army wouldn't dare touch it,
he said.

None of the roads to the South was blocked, he said. Every
time the army blew up bridges or put concrete blocks on border
crossings, the locals came out in force and replaced them. Under
the Emergency Provisions Act, the army had the right to occupy
land and houses at will, and this was what they were using now
in the outposts. They had built three outposts, but had lost more
than five men in the preparations; several army and RUC personnel had been injured as well. The outposts, Jim said, made
them very vulnerable. 'There would be little sympathy for a Brit
or an RUC man shot or blown up in this area,' he said.

We passed by a shop which was in the South; the doorway
itself was the border, the outside of the shop being in the North,
every entry and exit involved smuggling. We stopped at various
houses for short visits, Jim introducing me to the occupiers as
someone who might be around the area over the following week.
'Look at him carefully,' he laughed, 'so you'll know him.'

We drove past The Three Steps public house, where Captain
Robert Nairac was last seen in 1977; into Camlough, where
Raymond McCreesh – one of the ten men who died on hunger
strike – was buried; past a place where a British bomb-disposal
expert had been blown up. 'He wasn't much of an expert,' Jim
said. I held my breath.

We sat in the house of another Sinn Fein man, and talked
about history. They were constantly amazed, he said, at the high
moral standpoint from which condemnations of the activities of
the IRA were made. The Southern state was founded on much the
same sort of warfare. Men who later went on to become pillars

of Southern society had once conducted the most vicious, ugly and murderous campaign of terror.

One of the men we met described Crossmaglen as 'an inconsequential little town minding its own business, with an unusually large military presence'. The British army, according to Desmond Hamill's book *Pig in the Middle, The Army in Northern Ireland 1969–1985*, which I had in my rucksack, took a different view. The army fort in Crossmaglen:

> . . . overlooked the large market square (the killing ground on which seventeen soldiers had already died). From it escape routes for the Provisional IRA ran out like spokes of a bicycle wheel: four to the border only ninety seconds away and two north into the hostile territory of South Armagh. In the village flew the tricolour of the Irish Republic and the Starry Plough, and while the soldiers watched and checked the locals, the locals looked on them as an alien force.

Hamill's book gave an account of the aftermath of the killing of a soldier in 1977, which included celebrations in one of the local pubs.

> A week later one of the leading singers of that night set off to get married. He had to drive five hundred yards to the church and every hundred yards he was stopped by a very polite patrol who asked him to wait while his car was searched. A company officer recalled: 'it took him an hour and a half to get to church, and by the time he got there he knew exactly what was happening and why. It was something the locals had never encountered before. What they were used to were soldiers rushing into pubs, knocking glasses off the bar, grabbing people by the hair, rushing them into the fort, sometimes with bare feet across broken glass, shoving them into a chopper and without them having any idea what was going on or why they had been arrested. We tried a different approach.'

No one in Crossmaglen spoke to the army. No one served them in the pubs. Regular efforts were made to land mortar bombs into the army base from lorries parked near the centre of the village. It was hard for a stranger to get served in the pubs. Jim McAllister, after my first encounter with a Crossmaglen public house where I was treated like an undesirable alien, warned me to tell them exactly who I was as soon as I came in the door, to use his name and tell them that he said it was all right. Otherwise I would have difficulty getting a drink in Crossmaglen.

I took a walk along the narrow roads and byways which crisscrossed the border. Most of the time I was within sight of one of the new outposts. I knew the army were looking at me. They could see for miles. North and South. Their vantage point was a new weapon in the long struggle to tame South Armagh. The previous day, the IRA had tried to bomb one of the outposts, without success. The only sign of this now was a big hole in the ditch, with branches of trees blown here and there as though there had been a storm. I walked up the road to a farmhouse near the outpost at Drummuckavall. When I approached a woman standing in the front yard, she asked me where I was from. I told her I was from the South. 'Look at what your government has done,' she said, turning away from me. She blamed the Anglo-Irish Agreement for the outposts. She went back into the house.

The village was intensely quiet; hardly anything moved. (The draper asked me where I lived. Dublin, I told him. 'Dublin,' he mused, 'I hear there's a lot of trouble down there.') I became a regular customer in Paddy Short's public house. On my second day in Crossmaglen, I spoke to the man there who claimed to have been the first papist ever to sleep the night in Ballinamallard. He was doing a building job almost thirty years ago in the village where this year's Twelfth of July celebrations had taken place; a bed was found for him, and the landlady was ready to defend his right to sleep in the town, despite threats that her house would be burned to the ground.

Paddy Short, the owner of the pub, was behind the counter listening attentively to all of this. He didn't know that Ballinamallard was a Protestant village. A few weeks ago, he said, he got a phone call from the Gardaí in Castleblayney, asking him for assistance. A couple from Ballinamallard had gone south to Dublin on their holidays and parked their caravan in one of the seaside resorts north of the city, only to find that during a shopping trip the caravan was stolen. The travelling people had stolen it, the Gardaí discovered, and were now living in it just north of the border, but south of Crossmaglen. It was parked on the side of the road.

The problem was how to get the caravan back. The fact that it stood within the United Kingdom made no difference. The army, the RUC, or the UDR wouldn't respond to a request for assistance. This part of South Armagh was officially a no-go area. They would be afraid of an ambush. The couple from Ballinamallard were also afraid of the no-man's land wherein lay their caravan. The Gardaí in Castleblayney wanted to know if Paddy Short would take the couple to the site of the stolen vehicle. Paddy said he would.

When they arrived at his pub, they wanted him to drive in his car, as they were worried about being hijacked. Paddy insisted on sitting in the back of their car. There was a man beside him. Paddy told all three of them that if the police forces, North and South, could stop harassing the locals and get on with fighting crime, then Crossmaglen would be a happier place. The couple in the front warned him to be careful: the man beside him was a Garda. Paddy wondered what a Garda was doing in the North of Ireland.

They found the caravan. The next problem was how to get it back from the travellers. Paddy told them there was only one way. Get a few lads to come out with shotguns, wearing balaclava masks, and the travellers would get out as fast as they could. The woman in particular was aghast, and made disparaging remarks about bandit country, Indian territory. Paddy shrugged, and asked to be brought back to Crossmaglen. If they wanted their caravan back, that is what they would have to do. He heard no more about it until a few days later when a Garda rang up from Castleblayney to thank him for his help. Did they get the caravan, he asked. They did, said the Garda. Did they do what he told them to do? Paddy asked. The Garda didn't really want to say.

Another man in the pub asked me if, on my travels, I had done the pilgrimage to Lough Derg. I said I had. He had done it as well, he said, travelling on a bus as far as Pettigoe with a friend, both of them intending to do the pilgrimage. They had gone into the local hotel, however, and decided to let the bus go on the few miles to Lough Derg without them. They spent the weekend drinking and having a good time, while the others sweated it out on the island; they rejoined the pilgrimage when the bus pulled up in Pettigoe on the way home. It was a great pilgrimage, he said.

As we were speaking, a man arrived in the pub announcing that he had just stood and watched while the British army stopped an official van from the Southern Electricity Supply Board, which had no business in the North. When they opened it, they discovered it was entirely full of mixers and soft drinks, which were almost twice as expensive in the South, a commodity high on the smugglers' list.

Paddy Short told me that he was tired of people coming into his public house and announcing that the South, the Republic of Ireland, was finished. He knew the national debt was in excess of twenty billion pounds, he knew the levels of taxation were punitive, he knew the prices were high, but it was still a better place than the North, and he was fed up with hearing the contrary.

Captain Robert Nairac, when he was stationed in Crossmaglen, used to come into Short's pub. They would never serve him, nor would they sell him cigarettes, but he would stand there and talk to people. They always knew he was in the army, but they could never understand exactly what he was doing. Desmond Hamill explains his role in *Pig In The Middle*:

> He suggested (in 1974) that the problem was one of intelligence and not straight soldiering, for the IRA in Crossmaglen would not be beaten by the army 'out-ambushing or out-shooting' them . . . Complete dossiers should be built up on every man, woman and child in the area . . . What was needed was a good intelligence officer based in the area for at least a year. It would be a long-term intelligence operation, allowing him to build up little bits of information.

Two years later they let Nairac out, more or less alone, to collect intelligence. Up at the bar in Short's pub they recalled him. One man in the company had been in another pub, since demolished, in the village, the night Nairac first came to their attention. It was near closing time. There was a singing session going on, the

man on the platform was slightly drunk and mockingly offered
the microphone to Nairac, who was wearing his uniform. Nairac,
to everyone's astonishment, walked up to the platform, took the
microphone and began to sing. He sang a Republican song, 'The
Broad Black Brimmer of the IRA':

> But when Ireland claims her freedom
> The men she'll choose to lead 'em
> Will wear the broad black brimmer of the IRA.

They couldn't believe their ears. Another man at the counter
remembered the night when the company had stood up to sing
the Irish national anthem, 'The Soldier's Song', at closing time.
Nairac was standing beside him, singing it in Irish. He knew the
words in Irish.

When local people were taken into the army base for interrog-
ation, Nairac would often demand that they be released. He posed
as different people when he went further afield; he could imitate
accents, but not in Crossmaglen. He had a good singing voice
and was known particularly for his rendering of 'Danny Boy'. He
was nicknamed 'Danny'. On 14 May 1977 he went to The Three
Steps Inn which that night was packed with local people. He sang
two songs from the stage. Later, he went outside. It is unclear
what happened, but there were signs of a struggle in the car park
of the pub; bloodstains and further evidence of a struggle were
found across the border. The IRA claimed to have executed him;
and although several men were sentenced in the South to life
imprisonment for his murder, the body was never found.

*

Down in the Sinn Fein office in the square in Crossmaglen,
Jim McAllister was working hard. Every week he produced his
own sheet of local news, which he enclosed with *An Phoblacht*,
Sinn Fein's weekly newspaper. Jim was one of the five Sinn Fein
members on Newry District Council, and was active on behalf
of his constituents, who had come to view Sinn Fein as all-
powerful. A woman came in one day, for example, and asked him
if he could assist her in moving her dog from her own house to

a relative's house. She seemed to feel this was part of Sinn Fein's function.

Jim told me that most of the previous generation of his family had been hired at the Hiring Fairs. They were never held in Crossmaglen, he said, because there were no big farmers in the area, so local people would travel to other towns. When I went back to my lodgings I mentioned this to the landlady, who said that most of her mother's family had been hired as well, including her mother. The following day her mother came from Castle-blayney to visit. She looked like a woman in her late sixties. She had been hired only once, she said; she often pointed out the house on the road into Newry. It was awful. She had to feed pigs and clean out the pigsties, and the food was terrible. It was a subject she didn't want to dwell on. Times were better now, despite the Troubles.

On a Saturday morning, Tony O'Shea and myself set out from Crossmaglen to Forkhill, about seven miles away, where there was to be a singing festival. It was a windy day; the sky changed every few minutes from clear blue to white clouds, but it was warm as we walked along. We met a few young travellers, walking towards Crossmaglen, who told us they came from a camp further down the road.

The travellers were to be found all over Ireland now, camped wherever they were left alone. They were despised by the settled population, who called them knackers, tinkers. They were gener-ally – often wrongly – associated with drunkenness and stealing. The draper in Crossmaglen had told me that they caused havoc when they came into his shop, ten or twelve of them together. There was, in the intensity of the feeling against them, a sort of fear; they were a reminder perhaps that not too long ago a great number of people in Ireland had been cleared off the land and had taken to the roads. The travellers were increasing in numbers all the time due to the early age of marriage, and the huge families which were common among them. They were, in general, intensely religious, refusing to consider any form of contraception, believing in the power of the Church. Some of them had been housed, but most preferred a nomadic life. By and large they did not have a high regard for settled people. There were seven or eight caravans parked on a lay-by. The women kept away from us. But the children swarmed around, wanting to have their photographs taken, wanting to show us a new baby in one of the caravans. None of their fathers seemed to be there, just a few youths sitting in a van on the road. It was difficult, they told me, they had no water and they got nothing from Crossmaglen, they had to go ten miles for water. Men had come out with guns one night recently, they said, fired a few shots in the air to warn them to get out, go somewhere else. They had said they'd be back some night. The youths in the van seemed downhearted, depressed. They didn't look at me as they spoke. I wondered where the older men were. The children, on the other hand, were eager that we should stay and amuse them. They wanted to follow us, as though we were a pair of Pied Pipers, but we made them go back.

We came to a crossroads where there was another caravan parked, whose owner came running up to us to invite us in for tea. He was full of sympathy for us because we were walking. He knew what it was like to walk, he said. Suddenly, as he spoke to us his family began to emerge from the caravan. First a wife, and then a teenage son and teenage daughters followed by a load of children. We all trooped back into the caravan for tea. The man's wife wanted to know if I could write. I could, I told her. She asked me to write out a letter to a priest in Leitrim asking him to send a copy of her baptismal certificate, care of the post office in Crossmaglen. She was having trouble getting state assistance, she said, as her name was a common name among travellers. She was, I presumed, claiming social welfare North and South, like many others. As I wrote the letter, the children grew busy looking through my rucksack which I had left outside the caravan, but they didn't take anything.

*

We moved on towards Forkhill, past ten white crosses in memory of the dead hunger strikers, with a slogan saying 'My Brother Is Not a Criminal'. Huge mushrooms grew on the side of the road; and the blackberries were coming into season; this year's crop were large, juicy and sweet, due to the high rainfall. As we made our way towards the coast, a soft white light came into the sky, the day brightened. We passed a field on a hill which a number of workers and a JCB were trying to flatten; the air was full of the smell of raw earth.

Forkhill was like a fortress. An enormous RUC and army barracks stood right in the middle of the village; and up on the stark, bare rock above Forkhill was perched another base from which helicopters came and went. The singing festival was to be held in the local hall, which had a bar, and intervals in the singing would take place in a local public house. There would be no live music, no fiddles, pipes or drums: this two-day festival was devoted to the human voice, ballads, folk songs, come-all-yes. Many of the people in the pub waiting for proceedings to begin had also been at the Fleadh Ceoil in Ballyshannon. This was a small world of its own, where everyone knew each other, where age didn't matter, but the ability to sing or play was all-important.

The singers and the audience, as well as myself and Tony O'Shea, who had found accommodation in a nearby village, soon moved up to the hall, opposite the army base. The light was dim in the long room, as we settled down to listen to an afternoon's singing. Love songs were followed by songs about emigration, smuggling songs by songs about dead patriots. Most of the time the tone was sombre; they were songs of sorrow and regret.

I went out to the front doorway of the hall, where one of the organizers stood with a drink in his hand. He was looking at Slieve Gullion, the mountain beyond Forkhill. This, he said, was the most wonderful place in the world. Look out there. We stood there together as hints of darkness bore down on Slieve Gullion. He loved the way the light made the colours different every single day. There was nowhere else like it. That's why he hated the Brits being here, he said. They thought they had rights to stop you, and ask you questions, they thought they owned the place. They hadn't touched Slieve Gullion yet. He wouldn't be responsible for what he did if they put a base or a lookout tower on Slieve Gullion.

At one point later in the evening, I went out to the bar to get a drink and almost bumped into two policemen who had

come, armed with rifles, to investigate what was going on. No
one spoke to them.

Down in the pub there was more singing. There was a lull
after a song when suddenly the traditional singer Mairead Ni
Dhomhnaill, who was sitting near me, started singing. I had only
heard her voice on record, and had no idea of its strength. The
song was in Irish, a version of 'Roisín Dubh', or 'Dark Rosaleen',
which she had learned from her aunt in Donegal. She was sitting
on a stool; her eyes were closed, her voice seemed to play with
the song, expanding to its full power on the high notes and
deepening as the song went low.

At lunchtime the next day the festival resumed in the village
of Mullaghbawn. It had been a long night, made longer by a
party in two adjoining houses, one owned by the singer Len
Graham, overlooking Mullaghbawn, which had formerly been a
barracks. There was a large amount of drink in the houses, and
a different session in every room. There were even a few
musicians, banned from the events of the day, playing traditional
music. When we woke up later in the morning, a big breakfast
was waiting for us downstairs in the house, part of a new estate
in Mullaghbawn.

This time the singing was in the local GAA hall. The Sunday
lunchtime drinkers stood around, pints in their hands, as the
organizers called on people to sing. A man sang a song about
the river Finn:

> When the wind was west
> The sport was best
> On the lovely river Finn

A woman sang a song about the Falklands War. There were more
emigration songs. A man told a story. There was a song cursing
an informer. There were love songs:

> The flowers will fade in the cold and stormy weather,
> They'll droop their heads and they'll wither away,
> So let us be going from amongst those green bowers,
> Where we'll join in wedlock in sweet unity.

The Dublin singer Frank Harte sang a version of 'Johnny's Gone For A Soldier', with a slow chorus in Irish. A woman at another table started a harmony with him, and soon the whole room was singing the slow mournful air of the chorus: '*Suil, suil, suil,*' as the cigarette smoke rose up around the tables and the cash register rang out.

*

I wanted to go back to Crossmaglen because there was a football match that afternoon between the home team and Bellaghy. I convinced a man from Derry to drive Tony O'Shea and myself back to Crossmaglen in time for the match, which was to be held on the pitch just beside the army base. The army had paid a large sum of money to the GAA in compensation for taking a section of the GAA grounds.

Before the game began, the crowd faced the tricolour, the flag of the Irish Republic, in silence. A group of small boys placed themselves strategically on top of the shelter where the substitutes from Bellaghy waited to be called. I found a niche in the shelter, and observed the play from there. From early in the game it was clear that Bellaghy was the better team, although there were moments when both teams were so bad as to make the game almost embarrassing for the spectators. Crossmaglen didn't score after the fourteenth minute of the first half.

'Play on, don't even look at it,' they shouted from the sideline as the British army helicopter flew low over the field on its way to the base. Soon afterwards, a scuffle broke out after a Bellaghy player butted an opponent in the head. Suddenly another Bellaghy player was attacked from behind, and given a vicious kick in the leg. He fell over. The subs ran on to the field, ready to do battle. For five long minutes the battle raged on the field; kicks, punches, swipes were exchanged for knees in the groin and butts in the head. It was fierce, and right in the middle of it, as the fighting was at its most intense, a helicopter took off once more from the base and flew over the field. The army must have wondered what the natives were doing now.

As the soldiers flew towards one of the outposts on the border, the referee managed to bring an end to the fighting. But it broke out again, as easily as it had stopped, and continued as though they were going to finish each other off. When it quietened again, the referee decided to put one player off from each side and continue. The Bellaghy subs came back to the shelter.

'How did you do?' I asked the chap beside me. 'I did well,' he said. 'I gave a fellow a good clip on the ear and then I got my boot into him, I did well.'

At half-time, the small boys were told to get off the shelter and go elsewhere. But as the second half progressed, they returned to cheer for Bellaghy, who were eight points ahead, then nine points. 'Right, Gerry, up his hole,' roared the sub beside me, as the Bellaghy player approached the man from Crossmaglen who had the ball. The helicopter came back from the outpost in the last few minutes of the game and this time it flew even lower over the field. 'They're bastards, the Brits,' the sub beside me said.

The final whistle blew, and the small boys jumped from the roof of the shelter on to the pitch, running towards the victorious Bellaghy team. We got a lift back to Forkhill, and continued on our way to Jonesborough. We were coming to the border's end; soon we would be able to see the sea.

Just south of here, at a place called Faughart, we had come earlier in the summer on a Sunday to attend a ceremony in honour of St Brigid. It was one of those blustery days, showers of rain being followed by clear skies and sunshine in quick succession. To the south we could see the rolling fields of Meath, the great rich pasture lands, and out to the east we could see the sea. Everything was to be in Irish: the Rosary and the mass. Most of the people who had come spoke in Irish; many had travelled long distances. A notice on the gate to the shrine said that the gate had been donated by the Gardaí 'in honour of St Brigid'.

In front of the altar, which was covered with an ugly sort of glass house, was a field in which the healing stones stood. Each stone was said to have powers to cure particular parts of the body. There were two indents for knees in the stone marked Knee Stone, with the Irish *Cloch Ghluine* printed above it. The people moved from stone to stone, some of them in bare feet, rubbing their heads against the Head Stone, their waist against the Waist Stone and so on. Streamers of material were tied to the bushes and brambles around the stones, as an offering for luck.

*

The summer was nearly over now. Even on Sunday as we walked from Forkhill lorries were carrying fodder North for the winter. Jonesborough had once been the great centre for southern shoppers, with bus-loads arriving from all parts of the South, queueing for cheap drink and cheap electrical goods. It looked faded now as we passed; its boom was over. The shoppers went further afield, to Newry, or on to Belfast. There was a hotel on the main Dublin to Belfast road which we soon came to; it was just over the border on the southern side. We were still in time for dinner, followed by a good long night's sleep.

We walked to Newry the following day, past the customs post and the lines of lorries, along the main road. When I bought an *Irish Times* I read a small item of news which puzzled me. Two men, it said, both travellers from a camp in South Armagh, near Crossmaglen, had been shot in the legs by the IRA on Saturday night, and were both in hospital. The RUC said that the IRA was trying to hijack a van. The shooting was condemned by a Catholic priest. The location suggested that the two men came from the camp we had passed on the road. The shooting must have occurred, then, a matter of hours after we went by.

Jim McAllister of Sinn Fein would be in Newry that night at the monthly council meeting. He would be likely to know what had happened. We hadn't time, on arrival in Newry, to search for lodgings; instead we went across the town to the council offices, deposited our rucksacks at the door, and went into the council chamber, where the meeting had just begun.

One whole side of the chamber was empty as the two DUP councillors and their seven OUP colleagues were boycotting meetings in protest against the Anglo-Irish Agreement. The Catholic SDLP, with fourteen members, had a majority on the council, with five from Sinn Fein and two Independents. One of these Independents, who was a Catholic, was chairman, having been elected by the nine Unionists and the five Sinn Fein members who banded together in a most unlikely coalition against the SDLP. Thus the Unionists and the political wing of the IRA were working together in Newry before the Anglo-Irish Agreement caused the Unionists to withdraw. It was, to say the least, a peculiar situation.

The Unionist withdrawal left the Catholics to fight it out between themselves. The SDLP members wore collars and ties, and looked like schoolteachers, shopkeepers, middle-class men who had a stake in society. The five Sinn Fein councillors, on the other hand, looked hungry, lean, untidy. They had proposed a motion that the outposts on the border in South Armagh be removed. What caused these outposts to be built in the first place? the man from the SDLP asked. 'The murder and mayhem,' he said, 'which was caused by those who hold the mistaken belief that uniting this country can only come about by the bomb and the bullet.'

Jim McAllister stood up to speak. They didn't just want the outposts removed, he said, they wanted the entire British apparatus out of this country. The SDLP began to heckle him about shooting poor, defenceless people on the side of the road.

'They tried to steal the brass doors from the tabernacle in Creggan church,' Jim McAllister said. The SDLP stopped heckling and became curious. Creggan church was in Crossmaglen. The people in question had been camped at the side of the road for over three months, Jim McAllister told the meeting. Day in, day out they had been involved in petty and serious robbery, he went on. His voice rose.

'Go out to Crossmaglen and ask. Thieves are not welcome, and the IRA will stamp them out if no one else will,' he said. He explained that a group of travellers had been found on the altar of the church, trying to unscrew the doors of the tabernacle. He waved a small leaflet in the air as proof. When he sat down I asked him for a look at the leaflet. He handed it to me. It was a four-page document, the sort issued in Catholic churches on Sunday, with local news and announcements on the inside pages, and prayers and sermons on the front and back. The sermon this

time was entitled 'The Paradox of Christianity'. The leaflet also
contained sayings such as 'Do not mistake activity for achievement', and 'God is with those who persevere'; 'If you can't be
thankful for what you receive, be thankful for what you escape.'

The local news included the following:

> During the week an attempt was made by itinerants to steal
> the brass door from the Tabernacle. Luckily, they were sur-
> prised when they had only half of the screws taken out and
> so had to leave empty-handed. Parishioners, particularly those
> in the vicinity, are kindly asked to keep an eye out for anyone
> acting suspiciously near any of the churches (or houses,
> schools etc) and perhaps even to check on what they are
> doing. Not everyone comes to church to pray.

The IRA, it seemed, went out to the travellers' camp on Saturday
night to warn them to get out. But the travellers were ready for
them with bricks and stones; the IRA men were lucky to escape.
'The shooting,' Jim McAllister said, 'came as a result of an assault
on volunteers.' The IRA shot two of the travellers in the legs
while trying to protect themselves. The story seemed unlikely,
but one of the SDLP councillors from the Crossmaglen area later
told me it was true. He didn't believe it himself, he said, until he
went to find out. Whether it was true or not, two travellers
were in hospital with gunshot wounds, and the IRA claimed
responsibility. The travellers had cleared out of the area, and the
tabernacle was now safe from thieves.

After the meeting, the SDLP members invited Tony and myself
to come and have a drink with them in the hospitality room.
The Sinn Fein members refused to fraternize with their fellow
nationalists, or drink gin and tonic with journalists, but most of
the SDLP councillors joined us. A key was produced, the drink
was put on the table, whiskey, vodka, gin and mixers. After several
gin and tonics, I suggested that we should hit the road as we still
had nowhere to stay, since there was no hotel in Newry. The
councillors mentioned the three hotels there had once been in
Newry, as well as the three in Rostrevor and the three in Warrenpoint, all bombed now, or closed up. One of them went to the
phone and rang the Osborne Hotel in Warrenpoint, a few miles

from Newry on the coast, which was still open, and the SDLP councillor from the area offered to give us a lift.

As we drove along the dual carriageway between Newry and Warrenpoint, the councillor told us that he had convinced the Stormont government – who were desperate to appease the Catholic population without being seen to do so – at the beginning of the 1970s, that a dual carriageway between Newry and Warrenpoint was badly needed. It was a Catholic area; the carriageway was built.

*

I woke up early in the morning, and stood at the hotel window looking out at the clear blue sky over Carlingford Lough. The border continued through the water and came to an end further out at the lighthouse; there was no more walking to be done. Omeath, across the water, was in the South.

We took a bus to Newry and a taxi a few miles out to Bessbrook, which was once a linen town, owned by the Richardson family, who were Quakers. There was still no public house, no pawnshop, and no betting shop; the police had only operated in the town for fifty years. Before that, the Richardsons managed everything. Bessbrook had none of the ragged, piecemeal look of the usual Irish town. Everything was built according to plan, in squares of red-brick artisan houses. There was even a lake and a park. (George Bernard Shaw said Bessbrook was so boring that even the swans on the lake were dying of boredom.)

It was still quiet; the old houses were intact. A sign across the street said: 'Bessbrook Says No'. The factory was closed, and the last of the Richardsons was dead; the nineteenth-century dream was over. The factory was now the main British army base for South Armargh. Helicopters landed and took off day and night where once two thousand mill workers had been employed. People had come from everywhere to work here. The Richardsons employed Catholics as well as Protestants, but Protestants held most of the top jobs. If you lost your job, you lost your house as well.

There was a bowling green in one of the squares; two teams of four were playing. We sat and watched them for a while, until one of them came over to talk to us. After a while he asked us how we thought the eight players were divided. How many Catholics? How many Protestants? I looked at them, searching for clues in the clothes, the faces. I had no idea, I told him. There were five Catholics and three Protestants, he said. There were no sectarian problems in Bessbrook.

Had I seen the monument to the ten men killed in the Kingsmills massacre? he asked. It was close by. All ten men, shot on the way home from work, had lived around here, he said: the two survivors lived in the town still. The Catholic man who was singled out and told to run and the Protestant man who survived being shot. Richard Hughes and Alan Black. He told me where they lived. Alan Black's house was just beside the bowling green. Richard Hughes lived on the other side of town.

As I knocked on Alan Black's door, a woman came up the street and asked me who I was looking for.

'Alan Black,' I said. 'He's not here. He won't be back until after six,' she said. It was only five o'clock. The woman scrutinized both of us carefully. I told her I might call back.

The monument to the dead men: 'Innocent Victims, Murdered at Kingsmills, 5 January 1976', stood at the bottom of the street. The mid-seventies had been a bad time for murders in the North. In the few months before Kingsmills, five Protestants had been shot dead in the Tullyvallen Orange Hall on the border in South Armagh. Three members of the Miami Showband, travelling back to the South after a night's playing, were shot dead. People had been snatched off the street in Belfast and brutally murdered. The motive in all cases was purely sectarian.

Of all the killings in those years, Kingsmills stood out. The twelve men had been coming from work in the evening in a minibus when they were stopped. The killers wanted the one Catholic man to stand out; the others thought that they were going to shoot the Catholic, Richard Hughes, and they tried to shield him. The others were all Protestants. But the killers made Hughes stand out. They told him to run, and then they turned and shot the eleven Protestants.

Just the previous day two Catholics – the Reavey brothers – had been shot dead nearby and a third wounded. It seemed that a new and more vicious intensity had entered the sectarian war at that time.

I found Richard Hughes's house and rang the bell. The door was answered by a man in his sixties. He seemed frail and stiff. It was hard to know what to say. I had prepared nothing. I didn't know what to do as I stood in front of him. Yes, he said, he was Richard Hughes. I told him I was writing about the area. He shook his head before I had finished. He was polite as he expressed regret that he couldn't talk to me about what happened at Kingsmills. He had never spoken to anybody about it in the ten years since it happened. He wanted to make sure that I understood. Other people had asked him, a TV crew had once told him that they filmed him while he was out walking his dog, but he still wouldn't talk about it.

Did the resurgence of the sectarian killings bring it back to him? I asked. It did, he said, when he saw the news on the television, accounts of more innocent people being killed. The men who were killed were his friends, he said, shaking his head in bewilderment, the only arguments he had had with them were about horses and football. That was the worst thought, he said: that some of them had thought he had set up the shooting. 'Did you think they were going to shoot you when they told you to run?' I asked. 'What would you have thought?' he asked, his voice slow and deliberate. He didn't expect a reply. We stood there without speaking, until he broke the silence by explaining once more that he couldn't talk about it, he was sorry, he had never, ever talked to anyone about it.

He stayed watching us as we walked away, saluting us before he closed the door. It was after six now, but I still wasn't sure if I wanted to call on Alan Black.

*

When I knocked on the door, I was uneasy about the reception I would get. The man who answered was young, much younger than I expected Alan Black to be. I told him I was writing a book. He invited us in. He didn't say anything. The front room of the house was small and comfortable. There was a fire lit. A television and video machine stood in the corner. Tony O'Shea

sat in an armchair beside the window. Alan Black sat on a sofa
on the opposite side of the room. I sat beside him. He seemed
puzzled about why we wanted to talk to him.

I told him we had passed the monument to the men who
were killed at the bottom of the street, and someone had told us
that he was there that day as well, and I wanted to know about
it. As I spoke I had an urge to up and run out of the room, and
as I finished I wasn't even sure that he was the right man, he
looked too young. What did I want to know? he asked. 'What
happened?' I said.

He turned to me and smiled, shaking his head. He couldn't
tell me the story all over again. It was ten years ago. I said that I
understood. His wife came in and offered us coffee. One of his
sons, aged about fifteen, came in and his father warned him to
be home at eight. The son went out again. He could show me a
video, he said, of the tenth anniversary ceremony for the boys
who were killed. He called them 'the boys'. And a television
programme made on the tenth anniversary, he could show me
that too. He didn't want to see it; he had never seen it, but he
could put it on, and go out while I watched it. His wife came
with the coffee, and he rummaged through the video tapes until
he found the one he was looking for.

It was an amateur film of a church ceremony. Alan explained
to me that they had thought the anniversary would be a small
affair, but crowds had come. There was a sermon from a
clergyman who explained that he was at home that evening when
he got a message to tell him to go to the hospital in Newry. He
knew that there had been a shooting. When he arrived he began
to see the faces of local people, relatives of the dead men, all of
whom he knew. The picture began to make sense as more and
more of them appeared. Slowly, he realized what had happened,
having wondered what so many people from Bessbrook could be
doing in the hospital.

The film was shaky and often went out of focus, but we stayed
watching it. Alan held the remote control and asked me a few
times if it was okay for him to wind forward. He didn't go out,
as he had said he would. His wife sat across the room, watching as
well. The television programme began; it had been shown on

BBC the previous January in the *Spotlight* series. It told the story of the Reavey brothers, shot dead in a sectarian assault not far from Bessbrook the day before the Kingsmills massacre. They were Catholics. It showed their father saying at the time that he hoped there would be no retaliation. But there was retaliation, the following day.

The film showed Alan Black standing at the place where it happened, which was marked by a cross. It then cut to him in his house, sitting where he was now, telling the story of what happened. The minibus was stopped at a roadblock, and they thought it was the army, he said. They were ordered out and told to put their hands on top of the bus.

It was only when they were asked who the Catholic was, that Alan Black realized that there was something odd. The army didn't usually ask such questions. The two Chapman brothers tried to shield Richard Hughes, but eventually he identified himself, and was told to take off down the road.

Suddenly one of the gunmen shouted 'Right', and the firing started. Alan was hit in the stomach and he went down. 'It was a nightmare,' he told the interviewer, 'and I don't want to speak any more about that part, it was just a nightmare.' The room was tense now, the four of us kept our eyes fixed on the screen, afraid to look at each other. Alan was still holding the control. The interviewer asked him how he knew the others were dead. 'I knew I was badly hurt, and I knew the boys were dead because there was no sound,' he said.

His elder son, aged about seventeen, came in and looked around, then immediately turned and went back out again. 'Will I push it forward?' Alan asked me. 'No,' I said. We watched in silence as he told how he heard crying and someone saying a prayer, someone who'd come on the scene. 'I thought I was dying. I was frightened,' he told the interviewer.

His first memory was of pain, not just the pain of his wounds, but of knowing that the boys were dead. He had eighteen bullet wounds. 'I already knew the boys were dead, I knew they were dead.' He said that he goes back every year for the anniversary to the place where it happened. 'It's a terrible place really. Sadness doesn't even begin to describe it.' They thought Richard Hughes was going to be the victim. 'Richard was a gentleman,' he said. Up to then, he said, 'the Troubles were always something that happened in Belfast or in Crossmaglen'.

Alan was in hospital with Anthony Reavey, the brother of the two who had been shot the day before the Kingsmills Massacre. They became friendly; they talked about everything except what had happened. But Anthony died a month later, and that, Alan said, was very hard to take. They thought that they had both survived. The Reaveys and the Blacks still keep in touch; at Christmas they exchange presents.

When the programme finished no one could speak. Night was setting in, and the room was darkening. He asked them, Alan said, after they made the programme, if they were using techniques to make him talk like that. They brought him out to where it happened and filmed him there, planning to film the interview the next day. But something about the way he reacted made them change their minds. He didn't know what it was; maybe, he thought, it was because he was upset. They decided to film it immediately. Talking about it like that had depressed him for months, he said, which is why he had never watched the programme before.

Sometimes everything he saw in Bessbrook reminded him of what happened. Not just the monument on 'Heartbreak Corner', but all the children growing up now, coming from school, walking around the town, the children of the men who were shot.

His wife turned on the light, which lifted us out of the atmosphere of the television programme. We could face each other. On the tenth anniversary of the killings, Alan said, a journalist had come over from one of the 'quality' English Sunday newspapers to talk to him. In passing, Alan mentioned that he was opposed to the Anglo-Irish Agreement, as were most Protestants in the North. This became the main feature of the article. He found it deeply distressing that his political opinions had been made important by the fact that he had survived. In Bessbrook, or Newry, among his friends and associates, his views were not listened to any more closely because of what happened at Kingsmills, he said.

His two sons came back into the room. It was time for them

to go with Alan to look at the few greyhounds which they kept in a shed a few miles out in the country. The dogs had to be taken for a walk. He seemed to want us to come with him, to talk somewhere else.

As we drove down the square, we saw an old man crossing the road. I knew I had seen him before. He was the old man who talked on the television programme about his two nephews, Reggie and Walter Chapman, who had been killed at Kingsmills. He was on his way to Alan's house. Alan pulled down the window and told him that we'd be back soon; they had plenty to talk about, he said. The old man agreed. As he drove away, Alan explained that they had a dog which had come last in a race. Last, can you imagine?

The younger son went to the greyhounds, while his brother began to drive the car back and forth; he was learning to drive. Alan showed us a big black dog he was proud of. He thought it might go places. The dogs were a great hobby, he said.

Suddenly, a shout came from the car. 'Da, Da,' it was his son's voice. Alan ran down to see the car stuck on a heap of sand. His son couldn't get it free. He calmly told the boy to get out, and he sat in the driver's seat and let the car lunge back towards us. The son looked at me, and raised his eyes to heaven; he had nearly crashed.

When Alan got out, the son started again, reversing, going forwards, reversing.

Black clouds were hovering now as night was coming down. We still had to take the dogs for a walk. Alan left his two sons there, one to clean out the small shed, the other to practise driving. He took the black dog, the one he had hopes for, on a lead up the road. The dog was full of energy, bursting to be let loose. Alan said we'd just go down the road a bit. He said he would drive us into Newry afterwards. He was relaxed out here; his face had changed, and his voice. He had forgotten that he was a survivor.

picador.com

blog
videos
interviews
extracts